Greatest Women Poses With Cigarettes Galleria

50 Best 1940-2015

75 Years of Best Female Poses

Another Fine Photo Collection by Cory Mark Picklo ©2015

I0489209

About the author's exclusivity:

Over 45,000 photos of the most sensual and stunning women poses lighting, inhaling, exhaling and holding cigarettes were selected from 1940 to 2015.

50 of the best photos made it in to the final selection process.

Each photo was then manually re-cut, re-positioned, reshaped and re-centered uniquely, allowing for an intentional new expression and interpretation of the photo as an art derivative.

Finally, each photo derivative was then manually changed through a second array of alterations including color, contrast, shadow, brightness, tone, lens filter type and saturation.

Please contact c2cEverything Company or c2cEverything.org for questions, comments and considerations.

TABLE OF CONTENTS

I. Best french snaps & inhales

BEST FRENCH SNAPS & INHALES

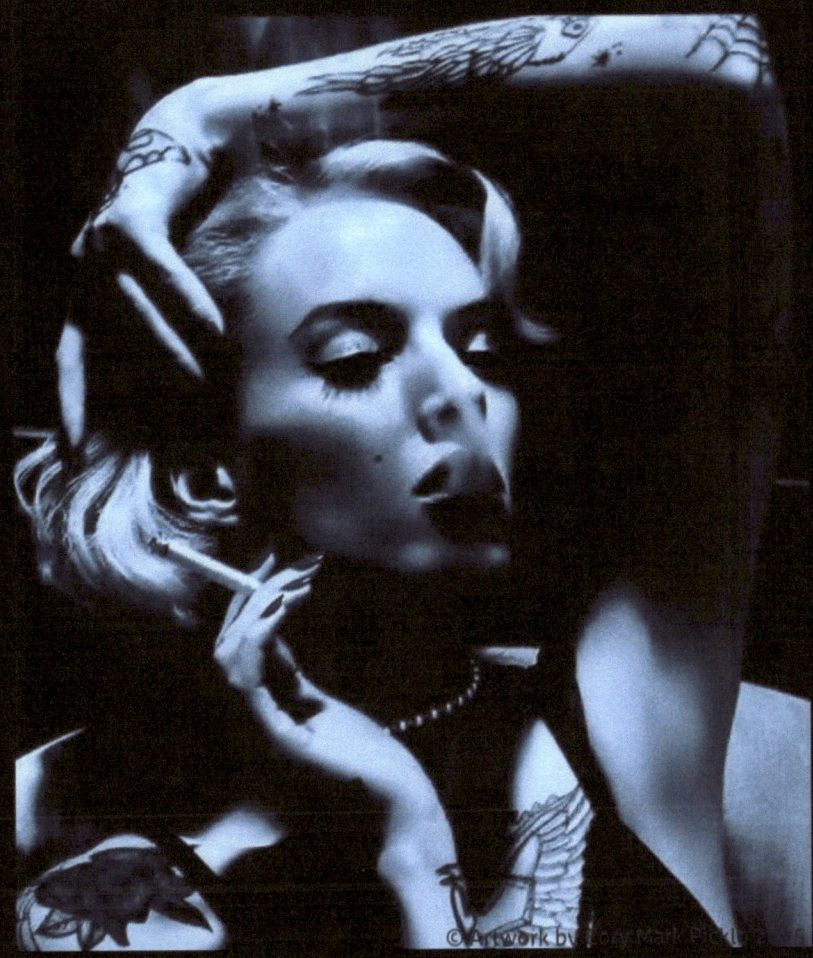

FRENCH INDULGENCE Artwork by Cory Mark Picklo Photography by Unknown, Creative Commons

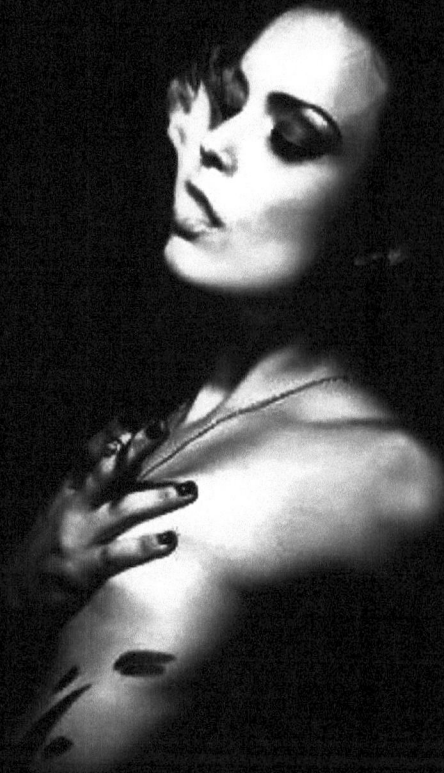

HEARTBEAT Artwork by Cory Mark Picklo Photography by Unknown, Creative Commons

BEST FRENCH SNAPS & INHALES

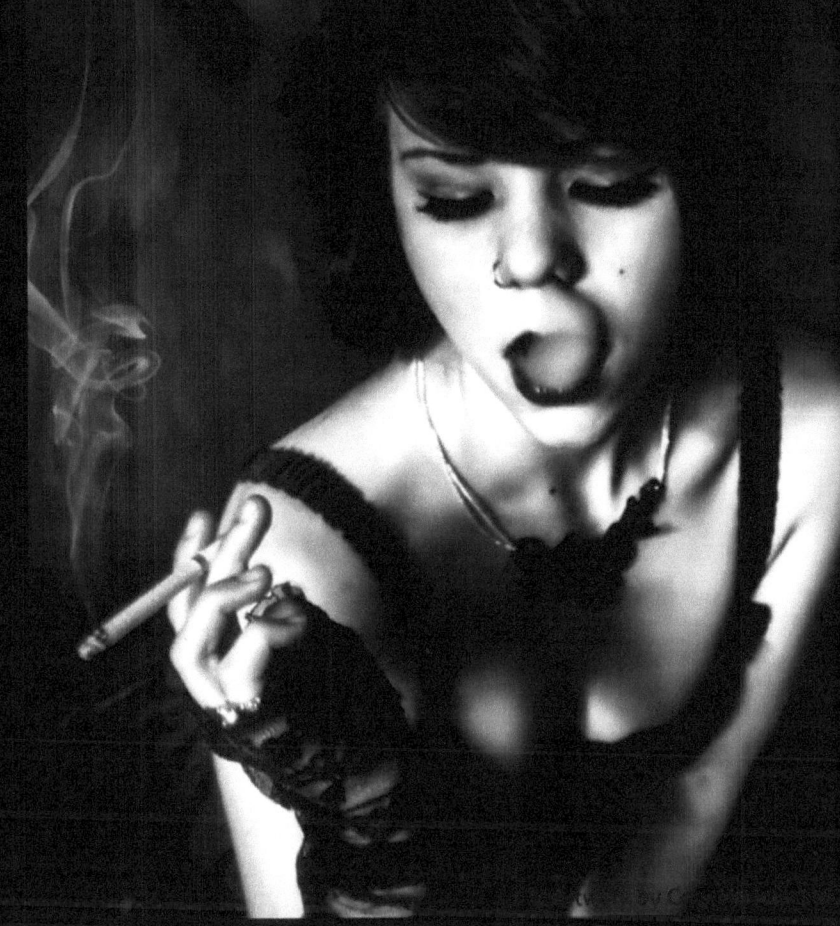

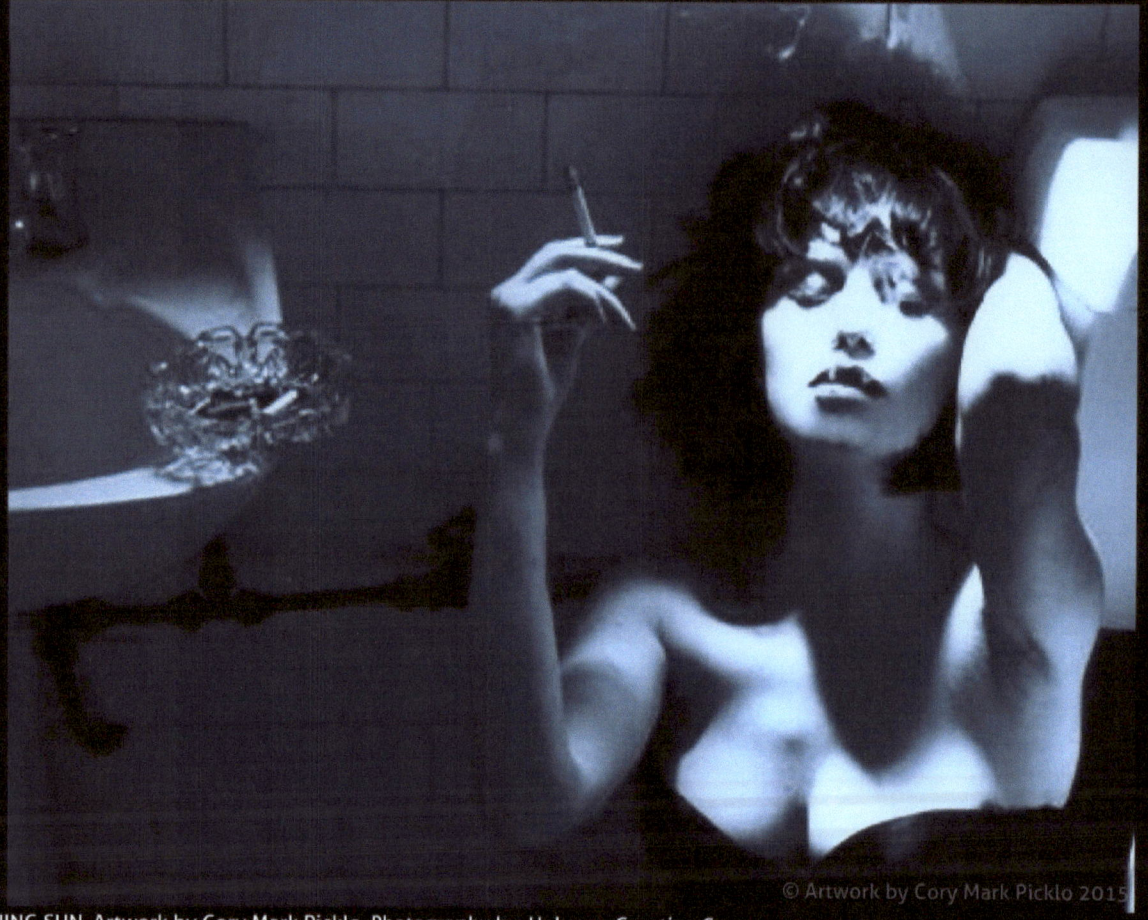

MORNING SUN Artwork by Cory Mark Picklo Photography by Unkown, Creative Commons

BEST FRENCH SNAPS & INHALES

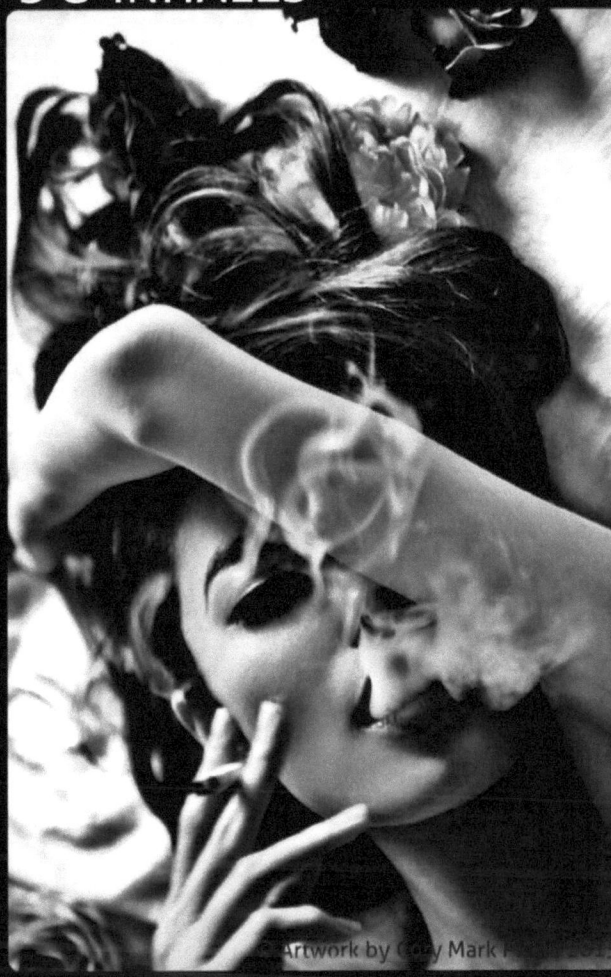

Artwork by Cory Mark Picklo 2015

OH ME Artwork by Cory Mark Picklo Photography by Unknown, Creative Commons

BEST FRENCH SNAPS & INHALES

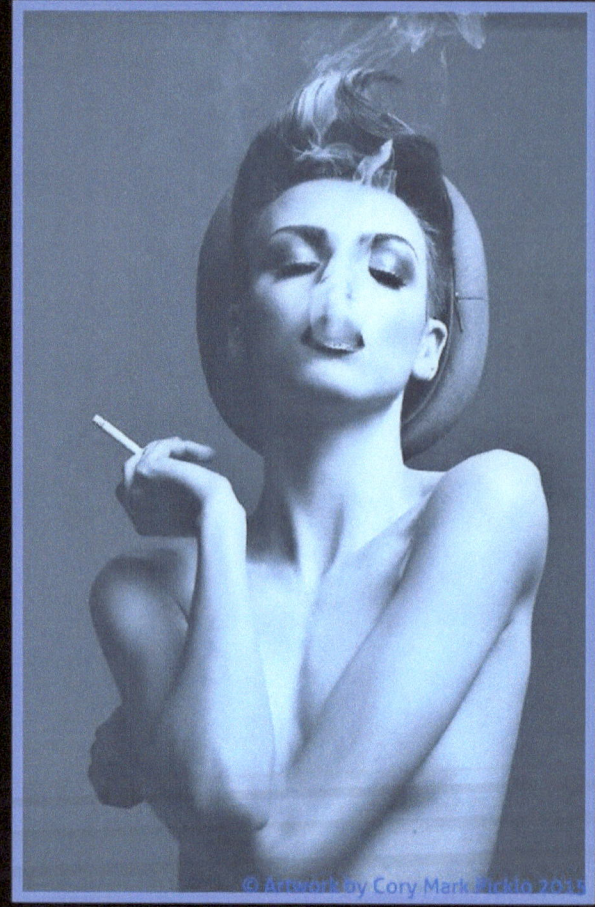

DESIR SEXUEL Artwork by Cory Mark Picklo Photography by Unkown, Creative Commons
P10

BEST FRENCH SNAPS & INHALES

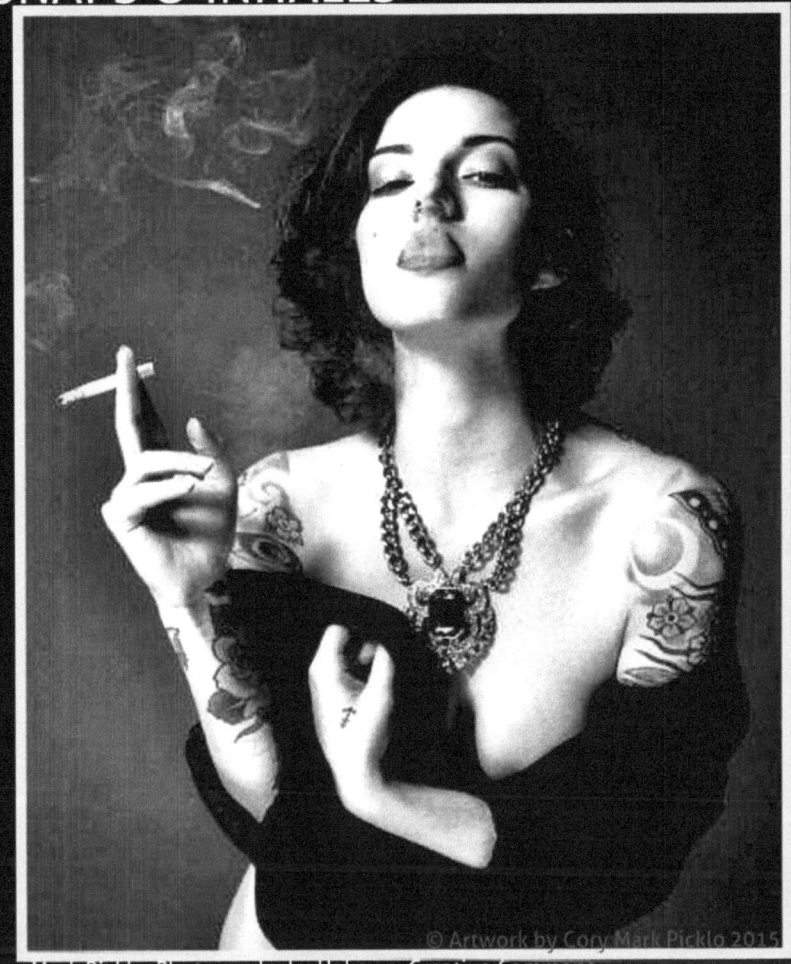

TEMPTATION Artwork by Cory Mark Picklo Photography by Unkown, Creative Commons

BEST FRENCH SNAPS & INHALES

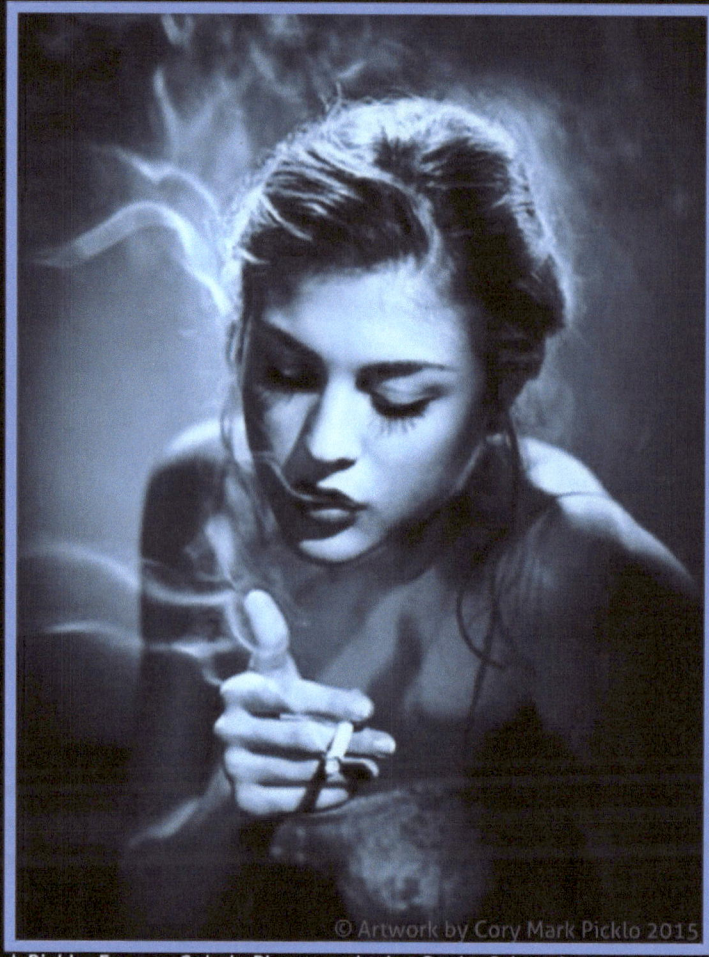

© Artwork by Cory Mark Picklo 2015

PRINCESS Artwork by Cory Mark Picklo Frances Cobain Photography by Rocky Schenck

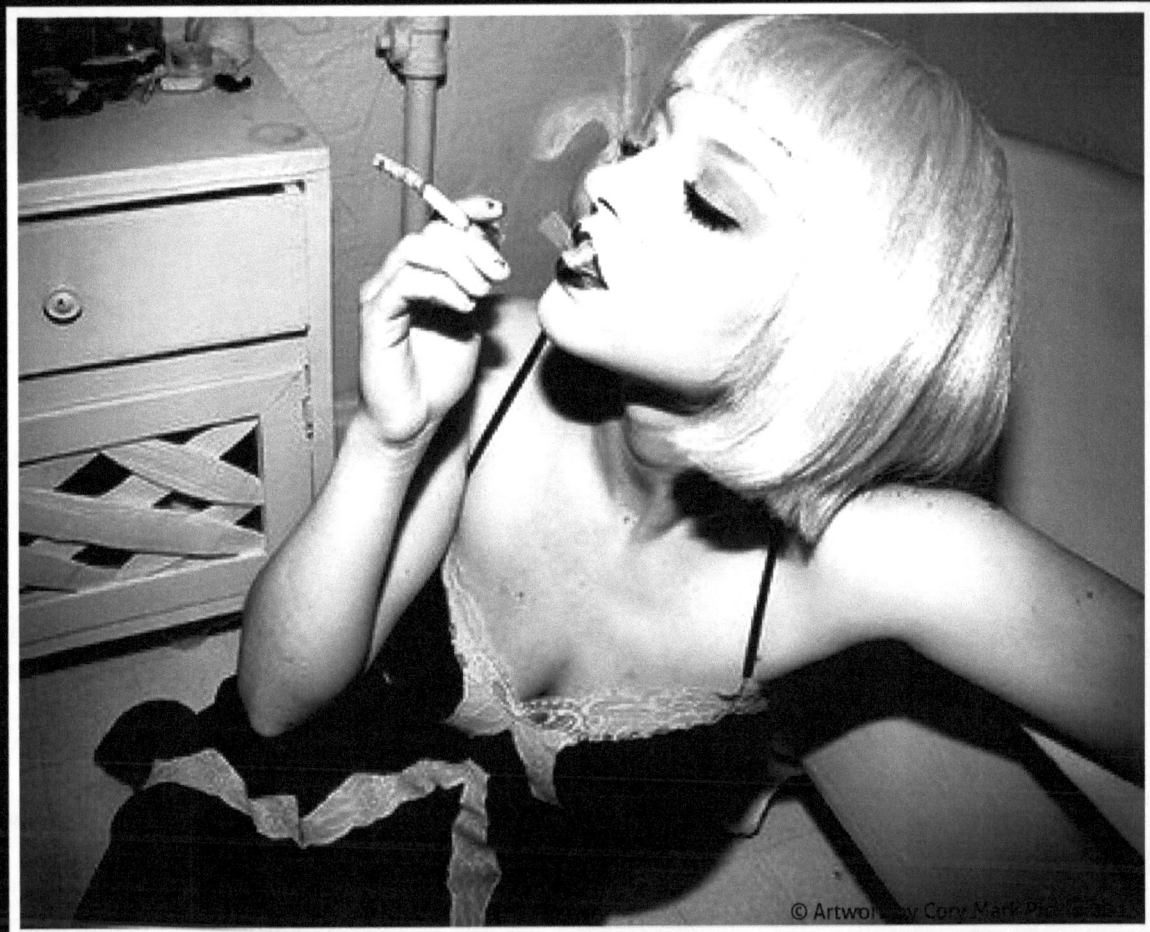

SEDUCTION Artwork by Cory Mark Picklo Photography by Unknown, Creative Commons

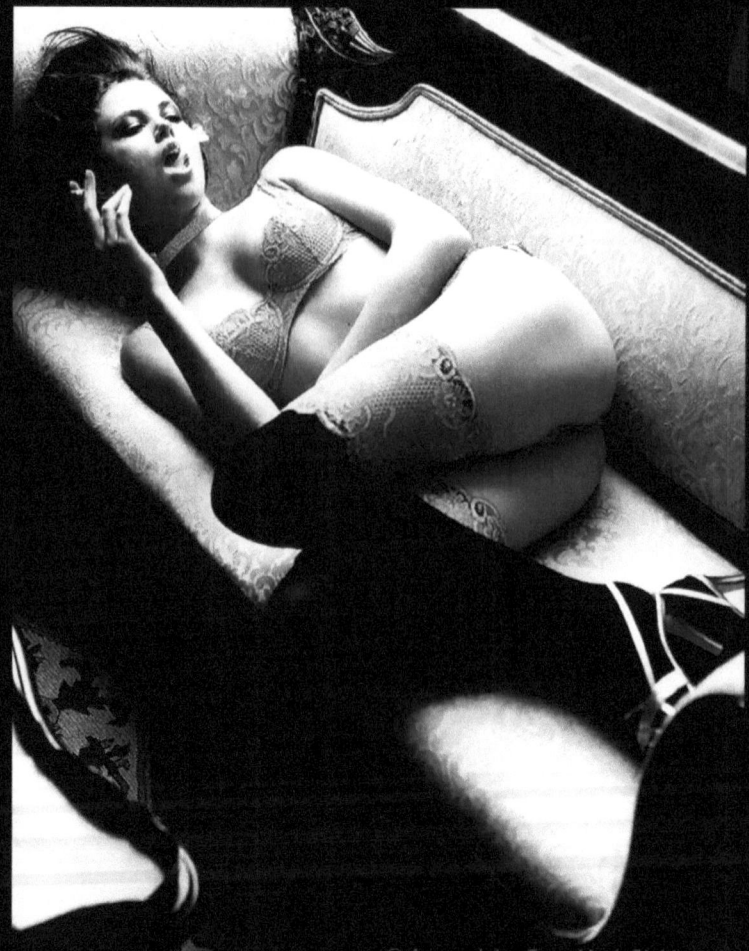

ME TIME Artwork by Cory Mark Picklo Photography by Unknown, Creative Commons

II. Best inhales

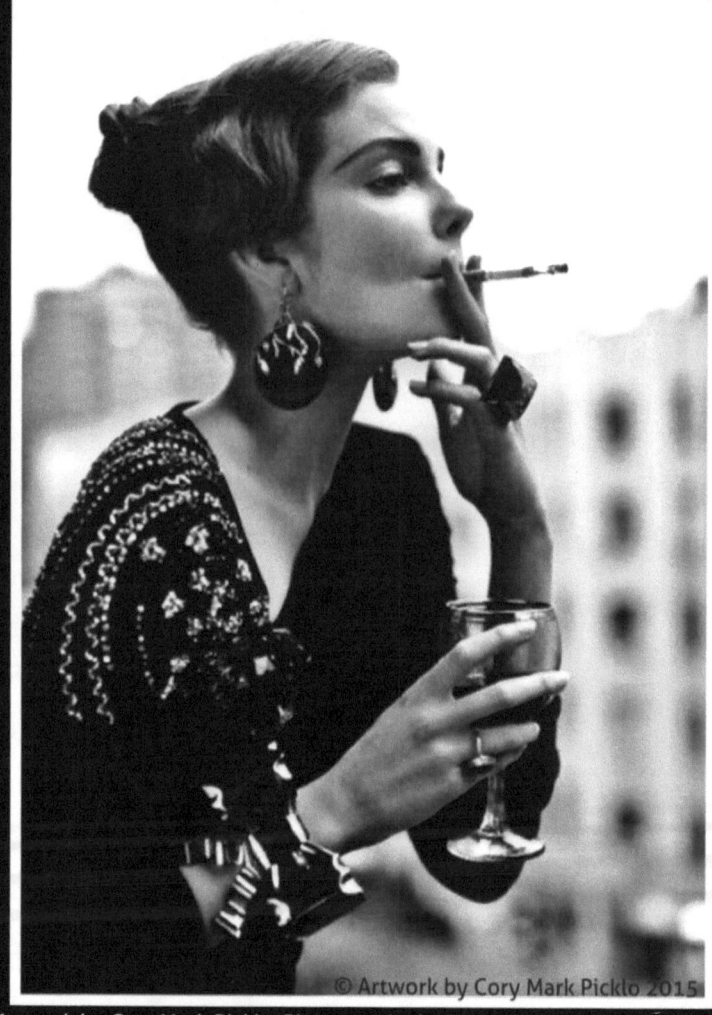

© Artwork by Cory Mark Picklo 2015

ELEGANCE & EXHILARATION Artwork by Cory Mark Picklo Photography by Town & Country Magazine
P16

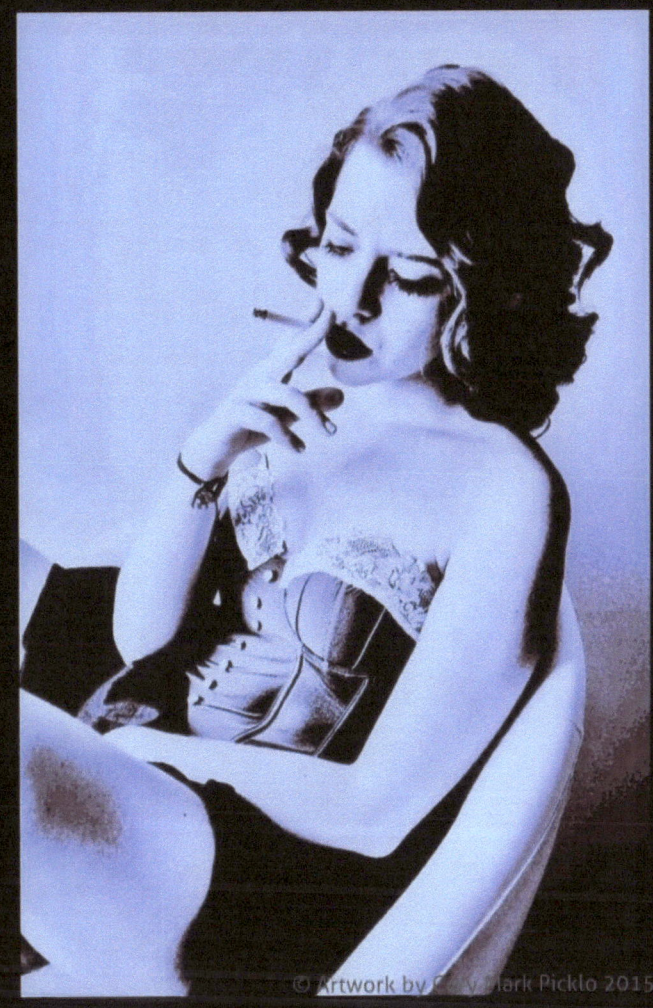

PONDERING Artwork by Cory Mark Picklo Photography by Creative Commons

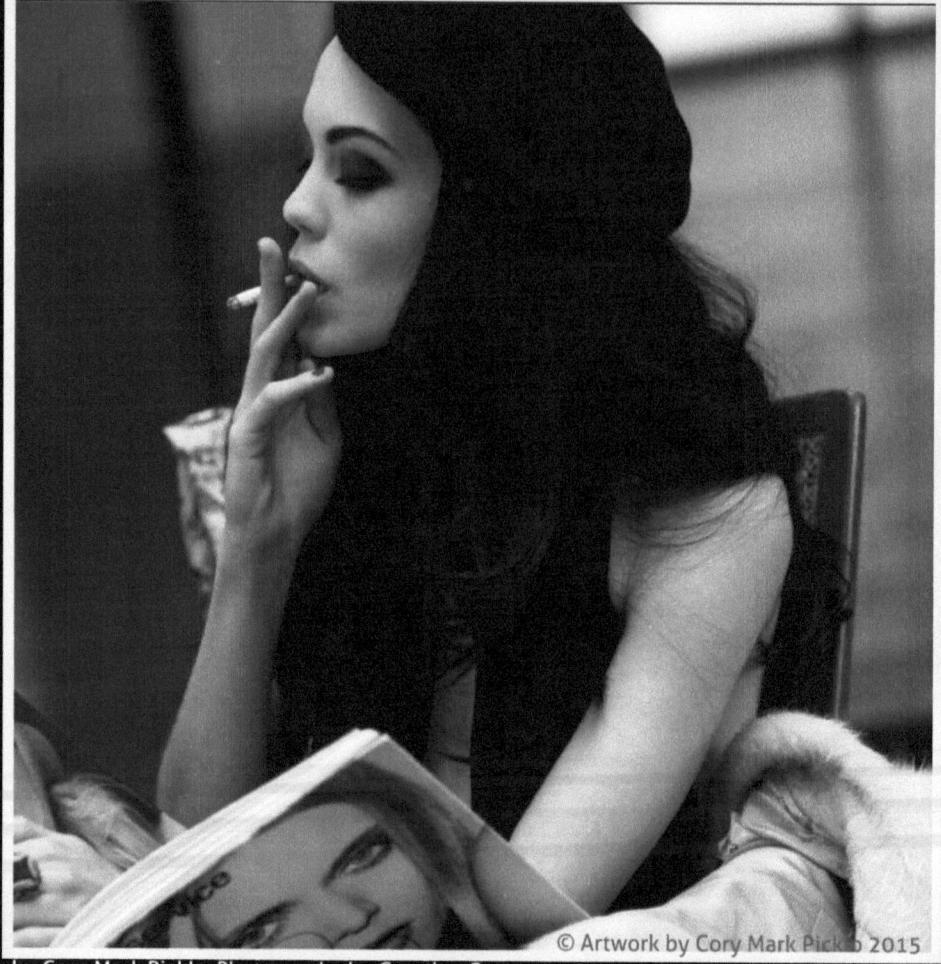

© Artwork by Cory Mark Picklo 2015

PERPETUAL IN Artwork by Cory Mark Picklo Photography by Creative Commons

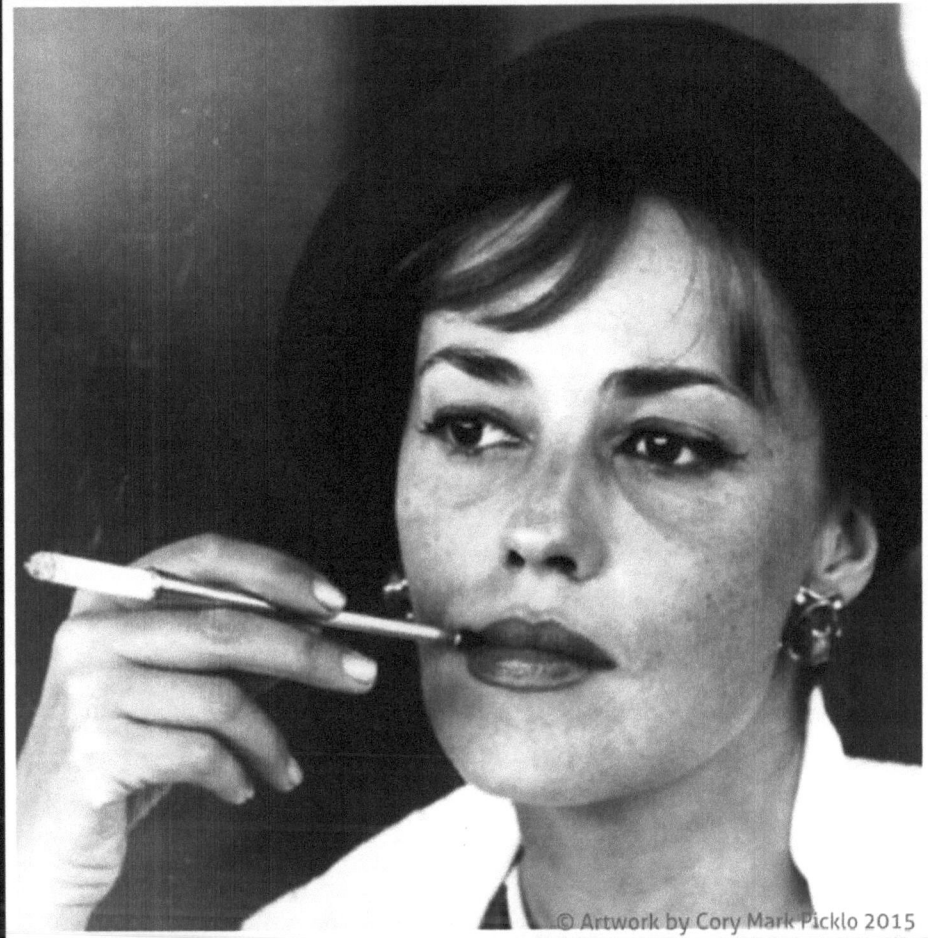

STUNNING BEAUTY Jeanne Moreau Artwork by Cory Mark Picklo Photography by Creative Commons

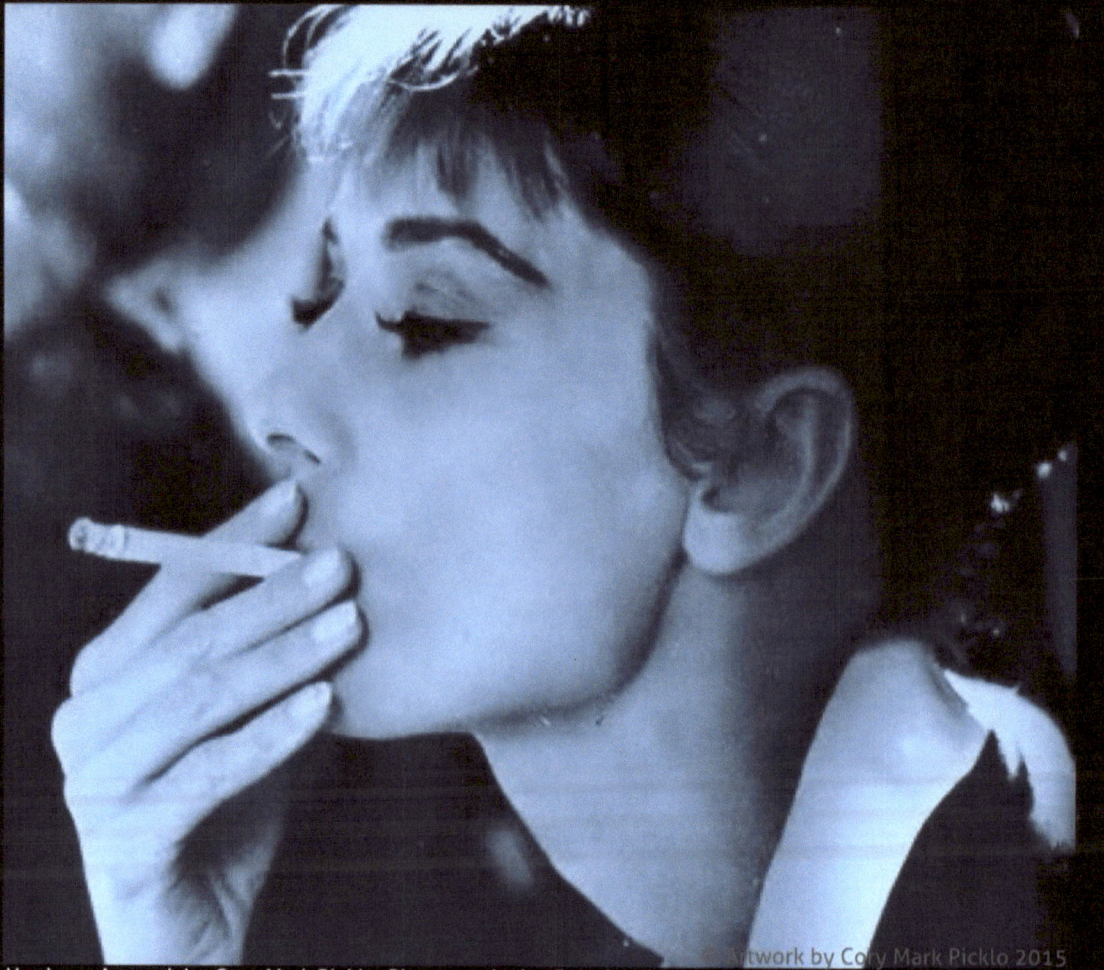

BLISS Audrey Hepburn Artwork by Cory Mark Picklo Photography by Creative Commons

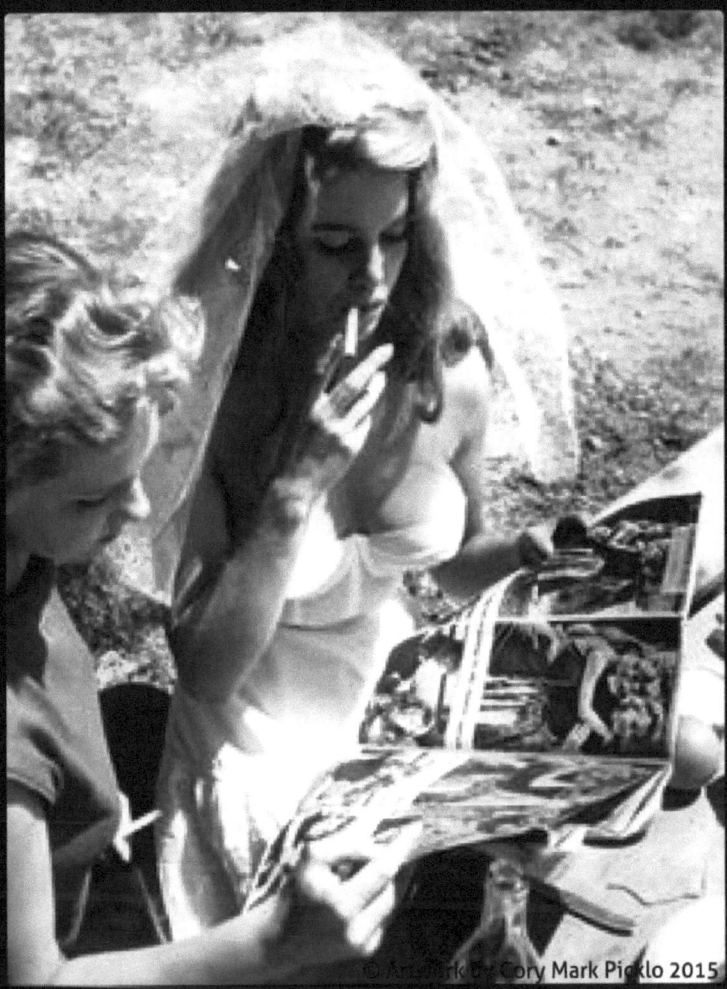

© Artwork By Cory Mark Picklo 2015

TAKE 5 Bridget Bardot Artwork by Cory Mark Picklo Photography by Creative Commons

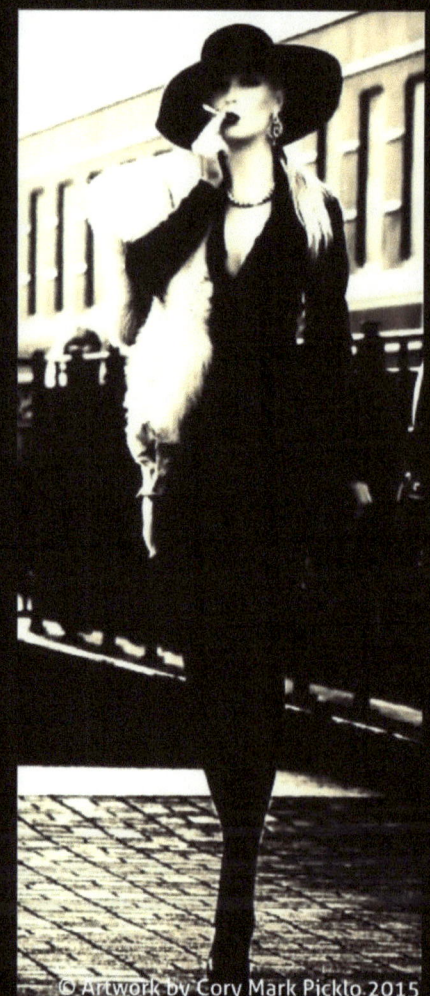

CLASSICALLY ASTUTE Artwork by Cory Mark Picklo Photography by Creative Commons

III. Best exhales

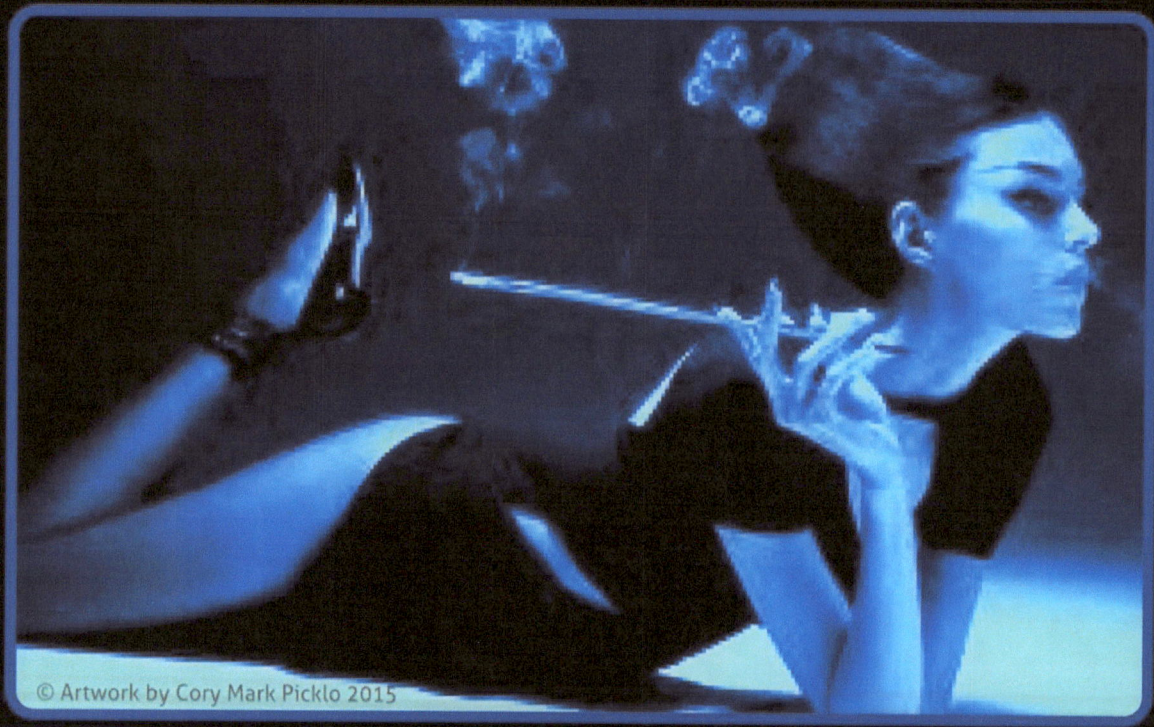

© Artwork by Cory Mark Picklo 2015

QUIXOTIC Artwork by Cory Mark Picklo Photography Creative Commons

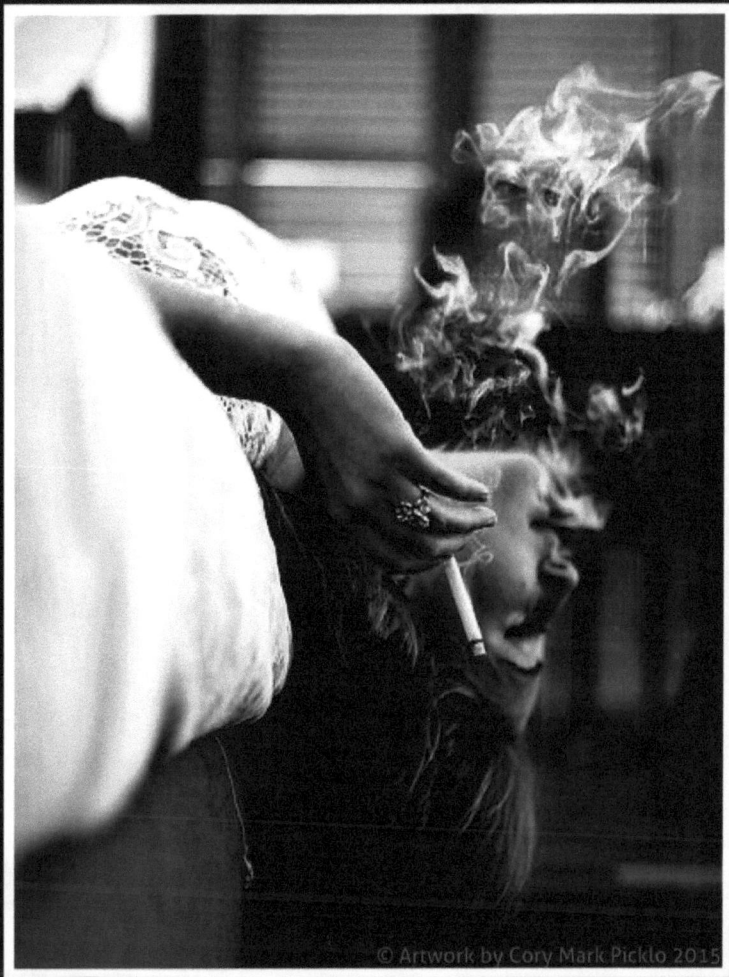

RELAXATION Artwork by Cory Mark Picklo Photography by Creative Commons

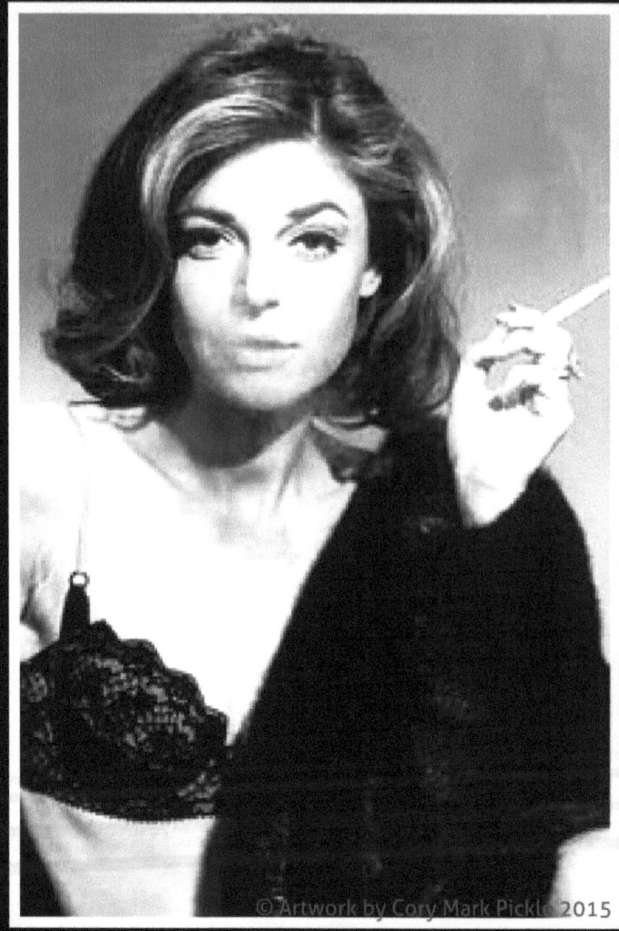

IN THE PINK OF THE HUNT Anne Bancroft Artwork by Cory Mark Picklo Photography by Creative Commons
P26

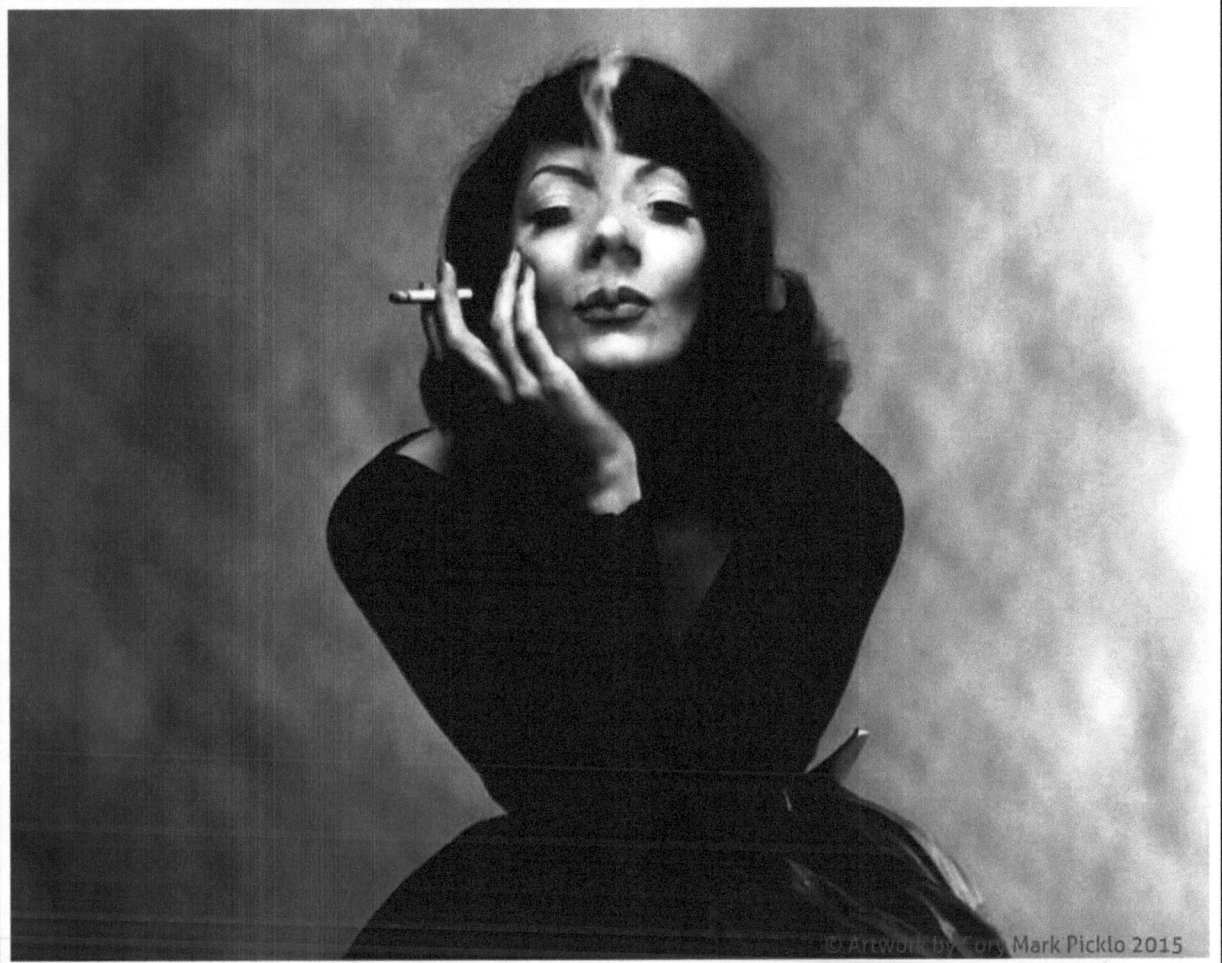

© Artwork by Cory Mark Picklo 2015

DON'T BE SHY Artwork by Cory Mark Picklo Photography by Jerry Schatzerg

IV. Best holding with holders

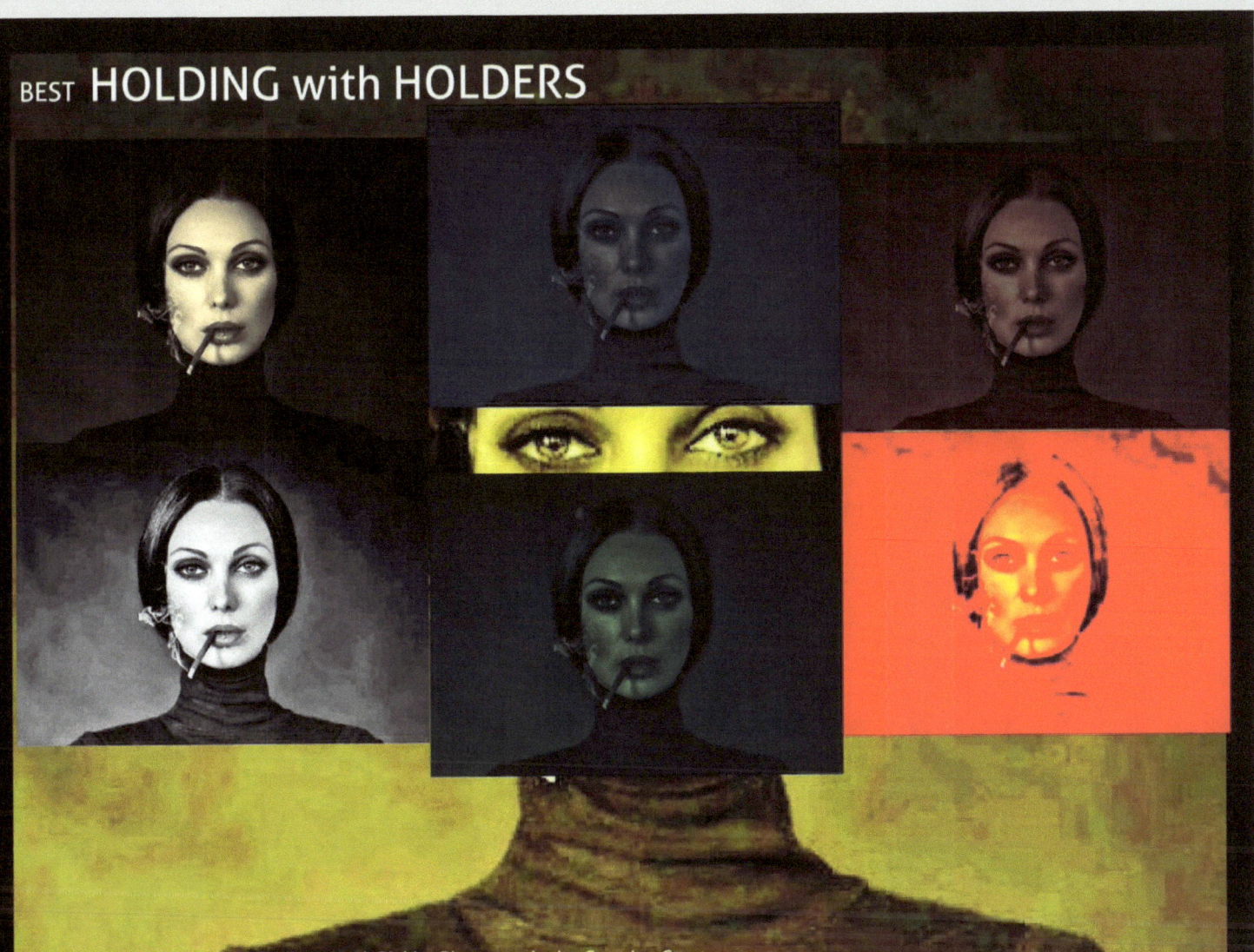

BEST **HOLDING with HOLDERS**

MY MANY MOODS Artwork by Cory Mark Picklo Photography by Creative Commons   © Artwork by Cory Mark Picklo 2015

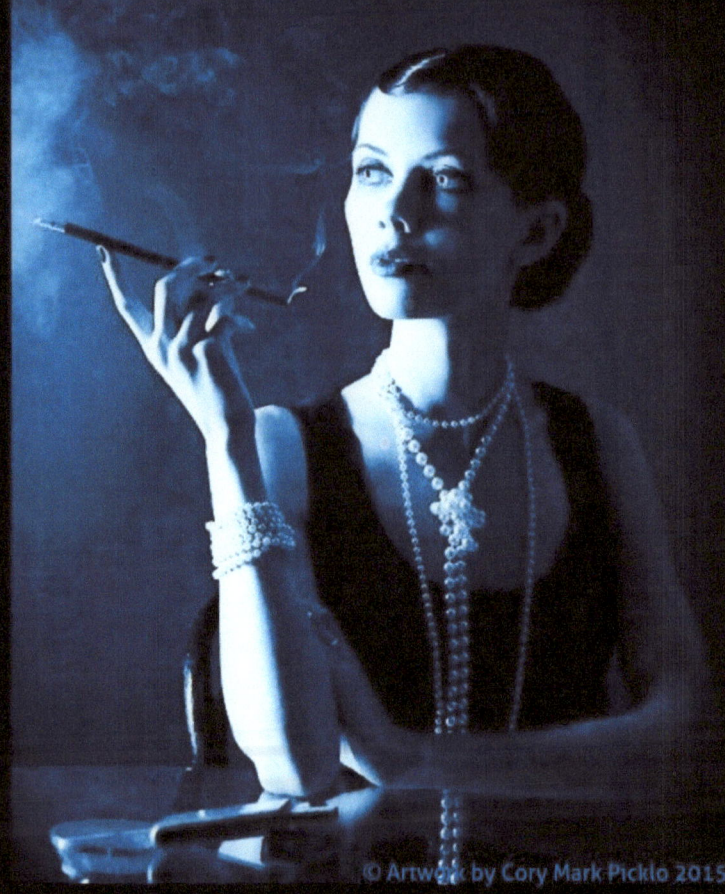

© Artwork by Cory Mark Picklo 2015

IMPERIAL Artwork by Cory Mark Picklo Photography by Creative Commons

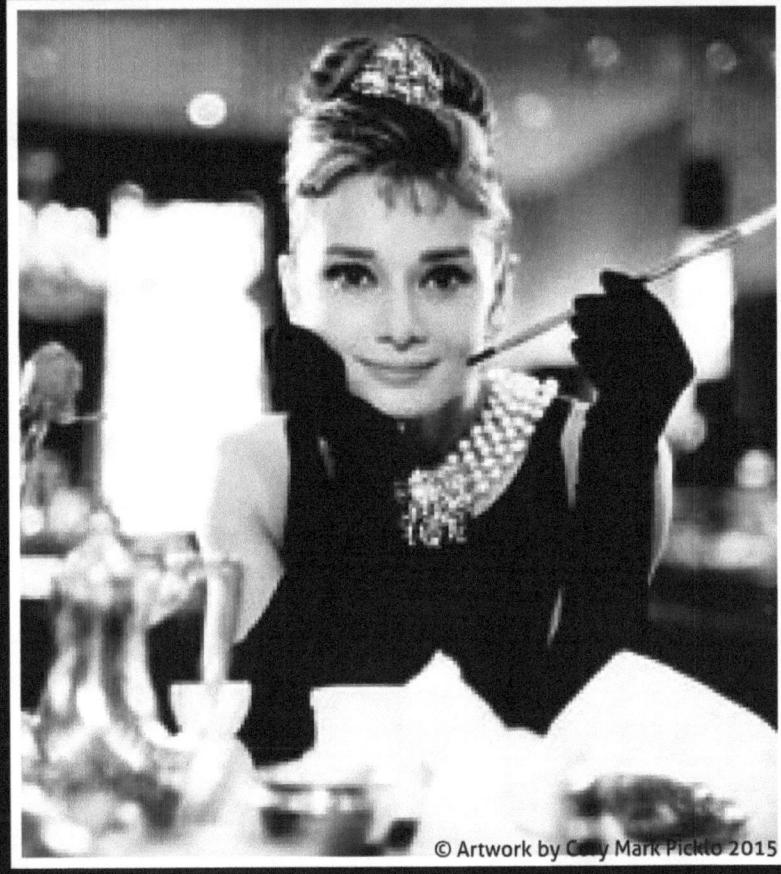

BON VIVANT Audrey Hepburn Artwork by Cory Mark Picklo Photography by Creative Commons

BEST HOLDING with HOLDERS

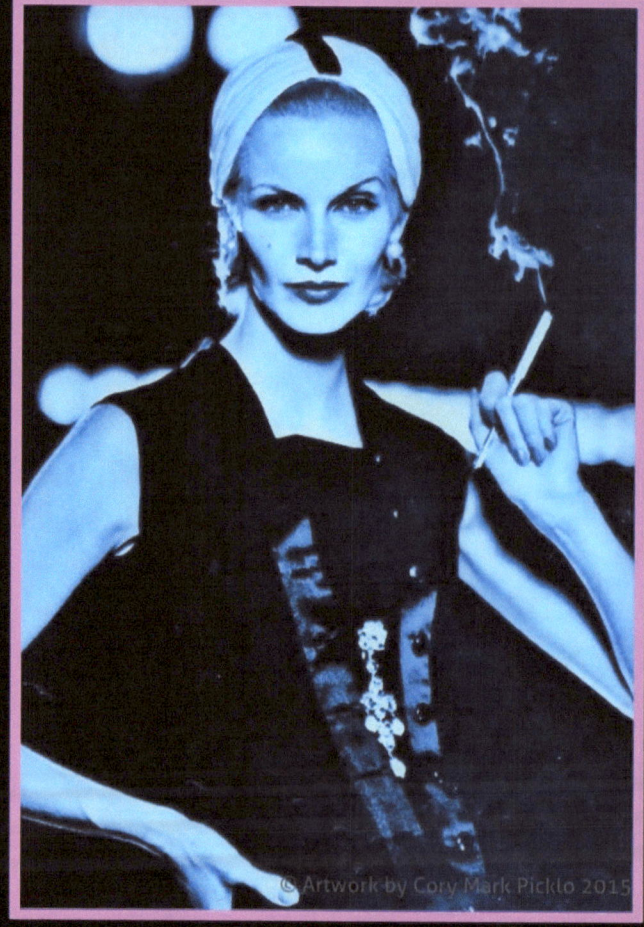

IN THE AGE OF AQUARIUS Artwork by Cory Mark Picklo Photography by Creative Commons

BEST HOLDING with HOLDERS

HUMANITARIAN STAR Audrey Hepburn Artwork by Cory Mark Picklo Photography by Creative Commons

V. Best holding

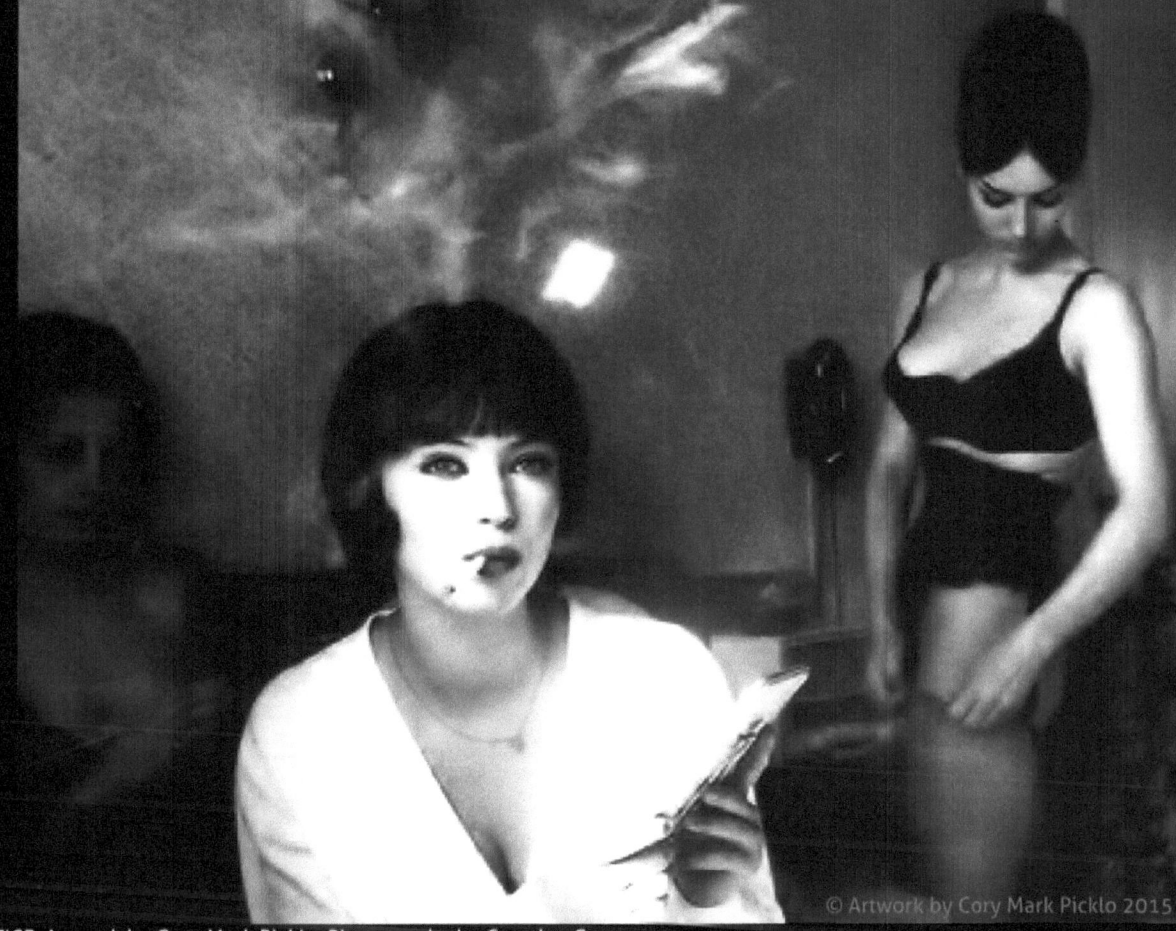

ENTICE Artwork by Cory Mark Picklo Photography by Creative Commons

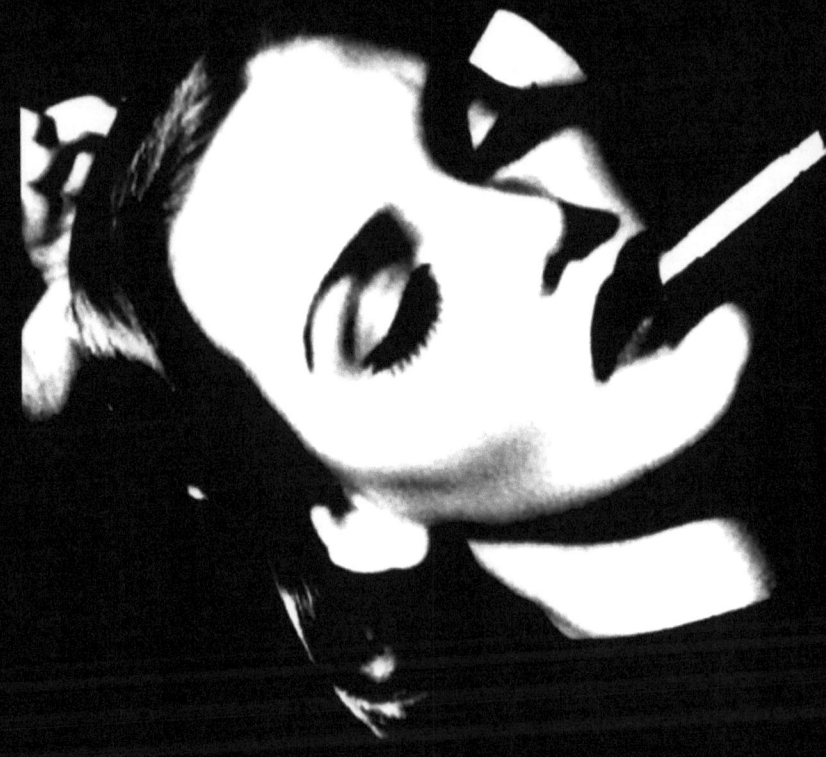

ALLUREMENT   Artwork by Cory Mark Picklo   Photography by Creative Commons

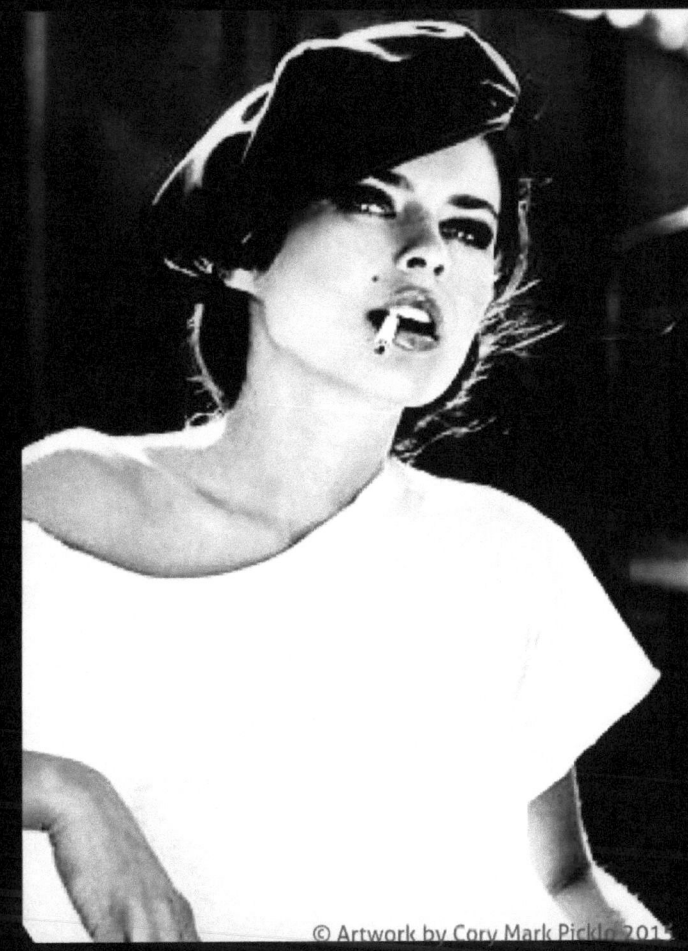

ENCHANTED Bridgot Bardot Artwork by Cory Mark Picklo Photography by Creative Commons

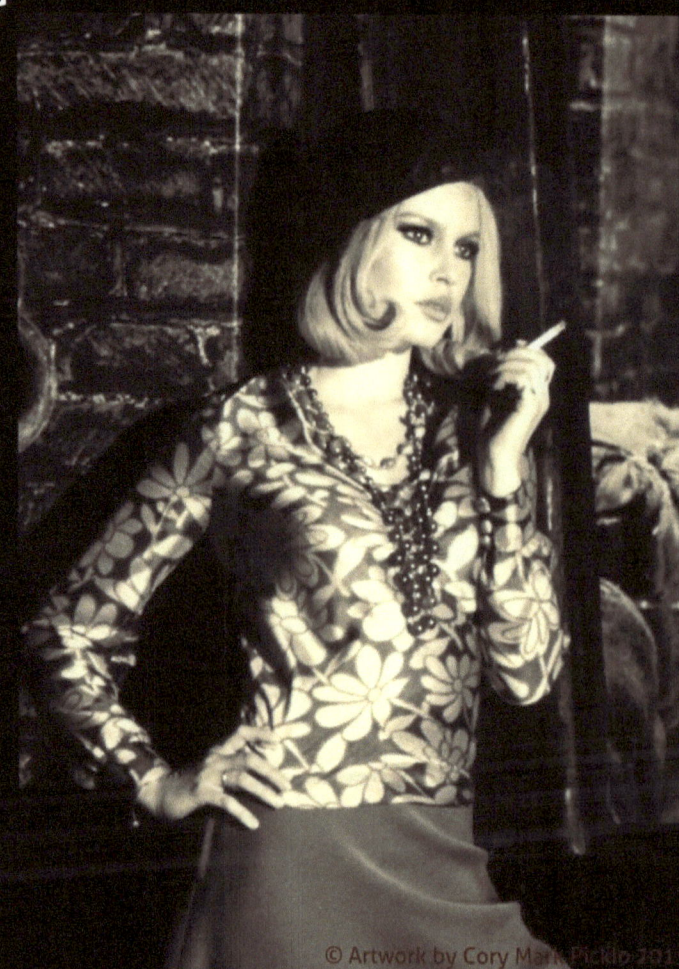

OBSERVATION Bridget Bardot Artwork by Cory Mark Picklo Photography by Creative Commons

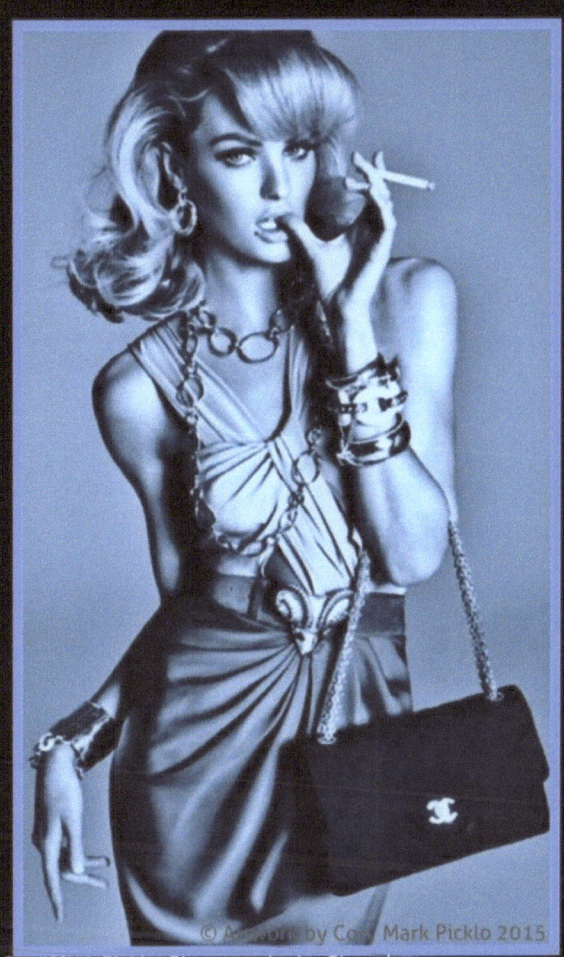

DRESSED TO IMPRESS Artwork by Cory Mark Picklo Photography by Chanel

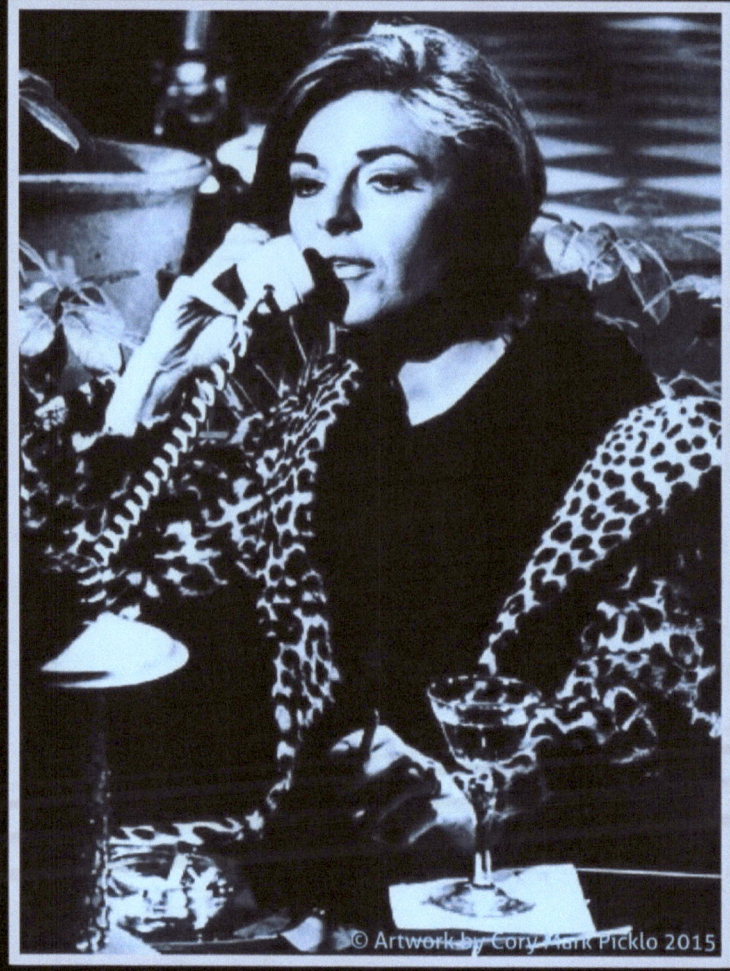

MEOW   Anne Bancroft Artwork by Cory Mark Picklo Photography by Creative Commons

BEST **HOLDING**

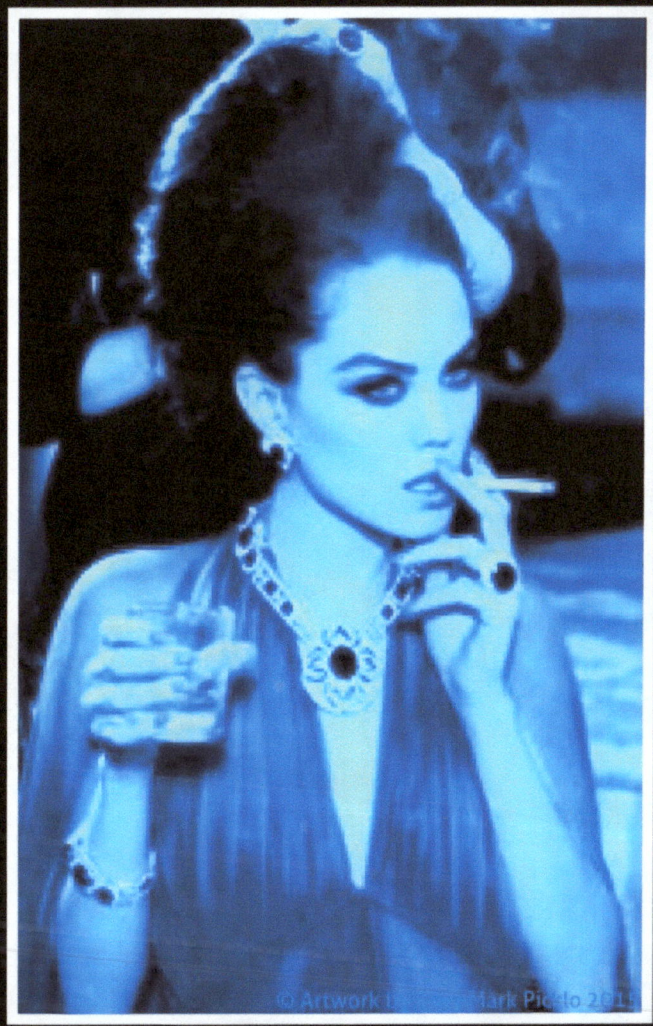

COOL PROWL & SOPHISTICATION Artwork by Cory Mark Picklo Photography by Creative Commons

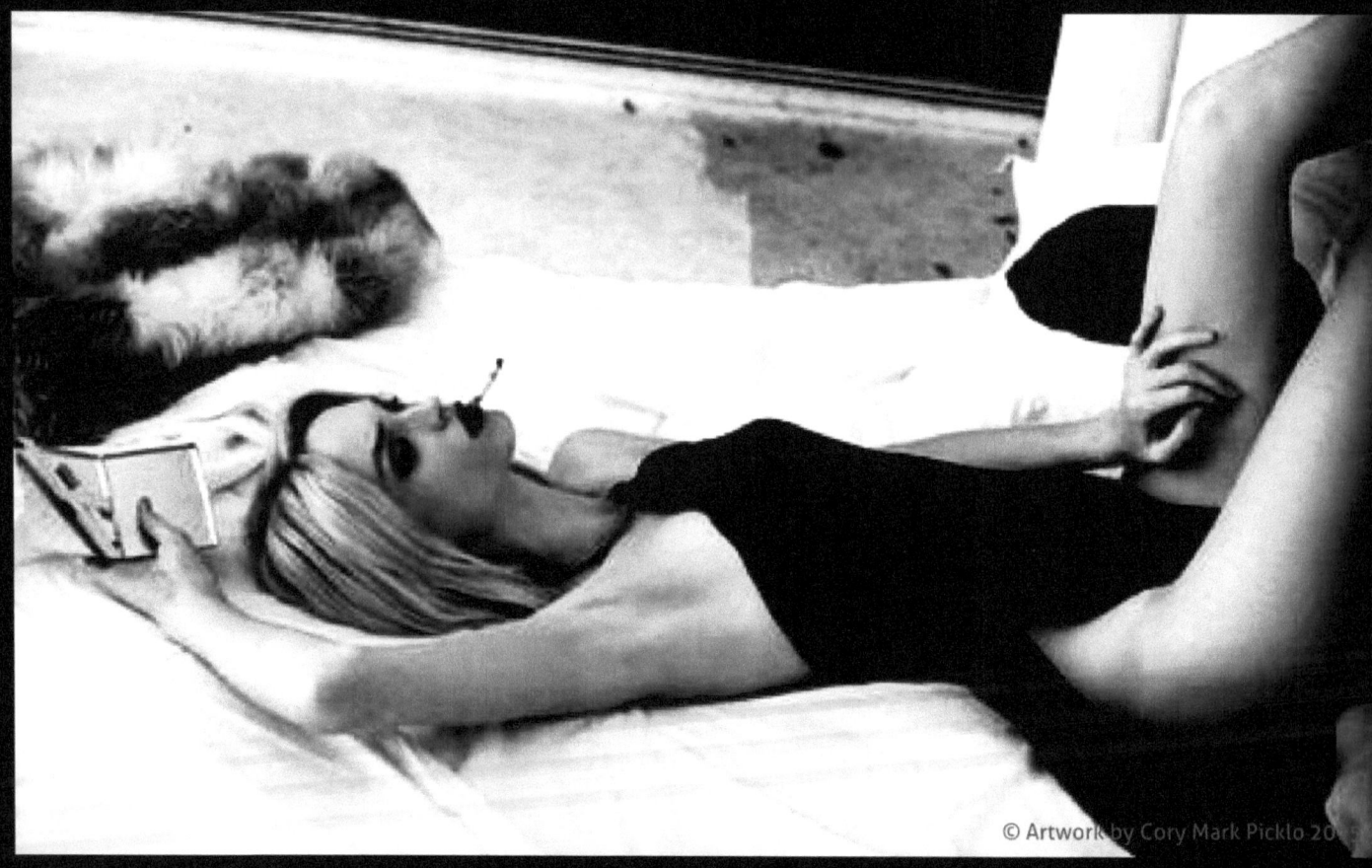

NOW WHAT Artwork by Cory Mark Picklo Photography by Creative Commons

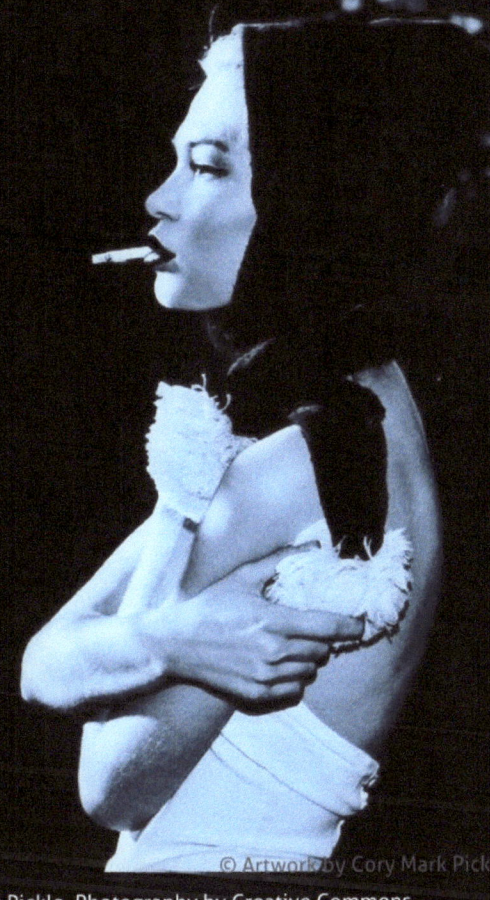

MERRY CHRISTMAS Artwork by Cory Mark Picklo Photography by Creative Commons

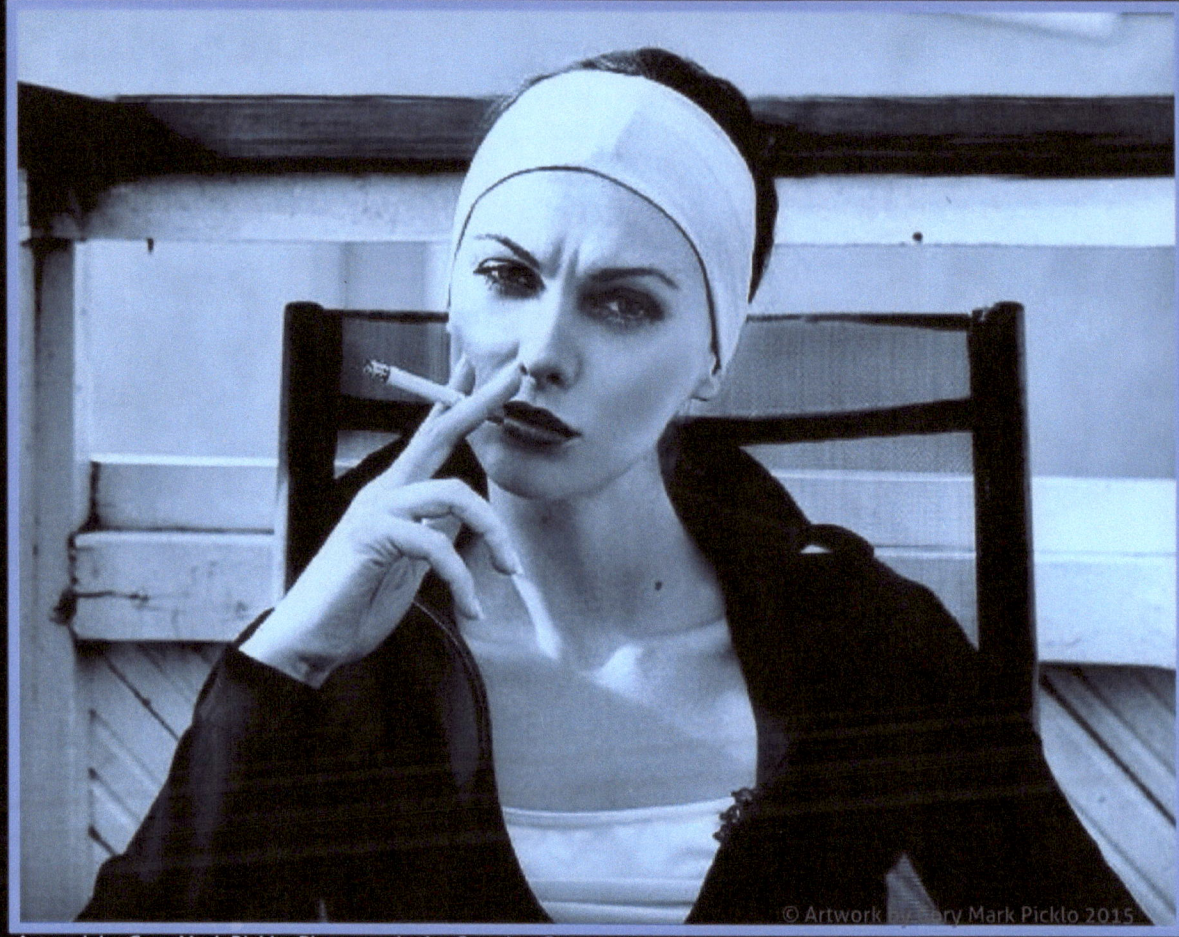

STUNNING   Artwork by Cory Mark Picklo Photography by Creative Commons

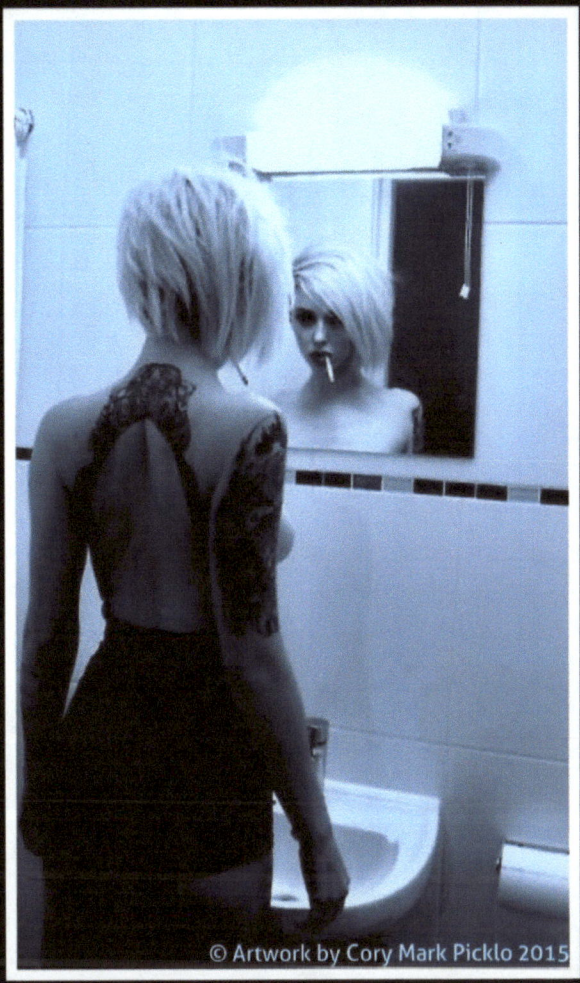

MAGNIFICANT Artwork by Cory Mark Picklo Photography by Creative Commons

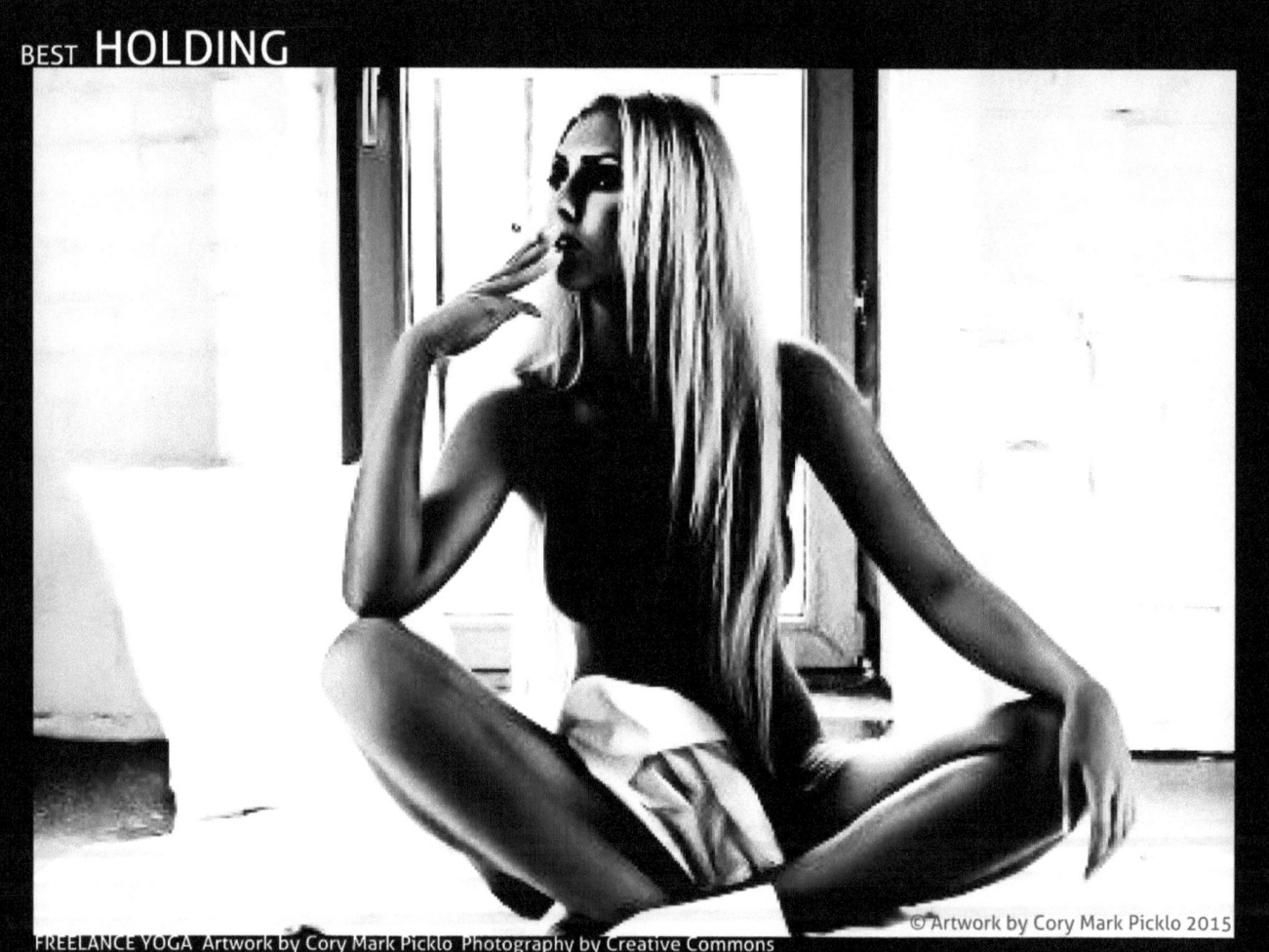

FREELANCE YOGA Artwork by Cory Mark Picklo Photography by Creative Commons

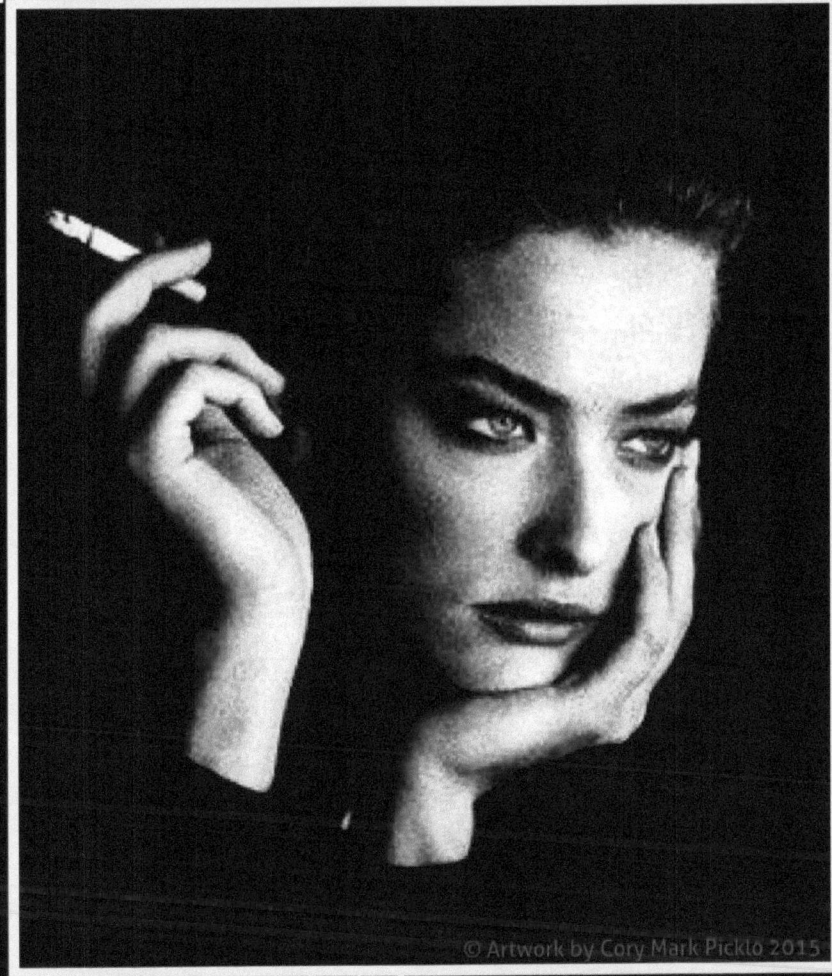

TRANCE Artwork by Cory Mark Picklo Photography by Creative Commons

BEST **HOLDING**

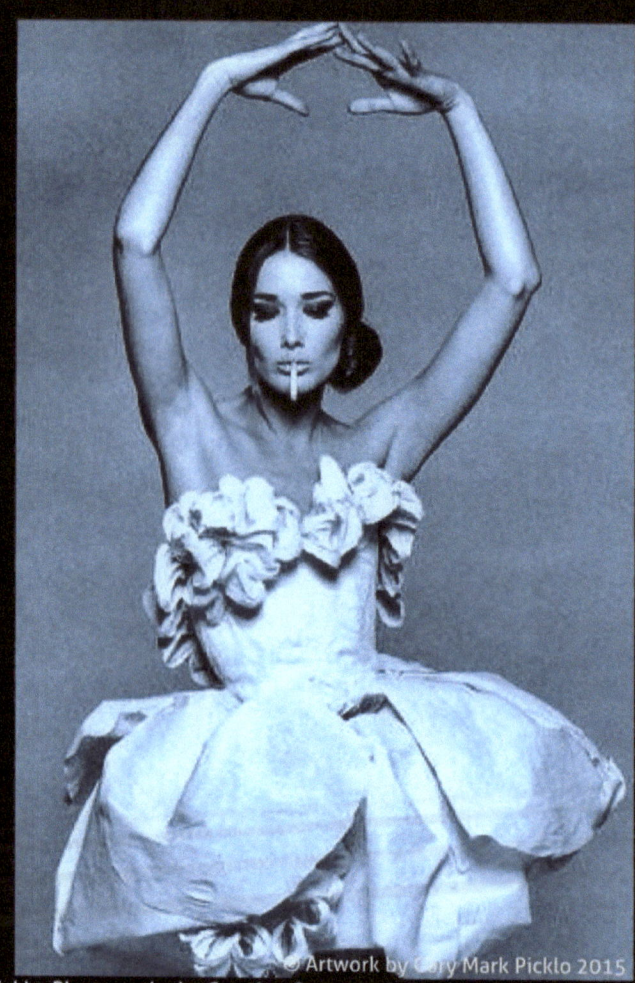

BALLERINA Artwork by Cory Mark Picklo Photography by Creative Commons

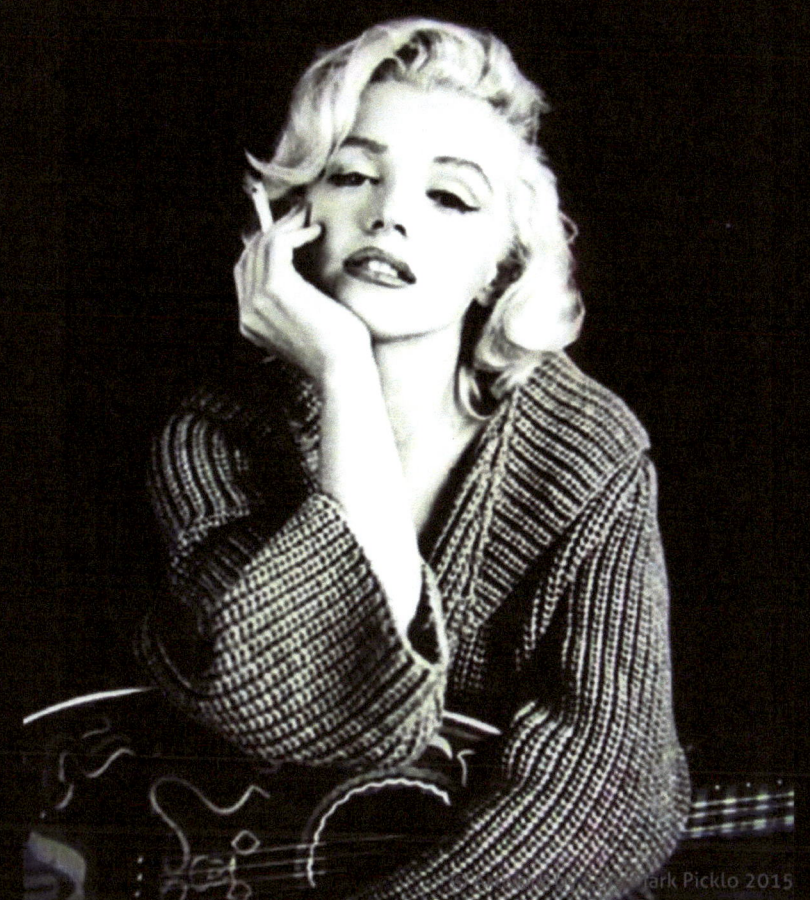

DREAMY GAZE Marilyn Monroe Artwork by Cory Mark Picklo Photography by Milton Greene

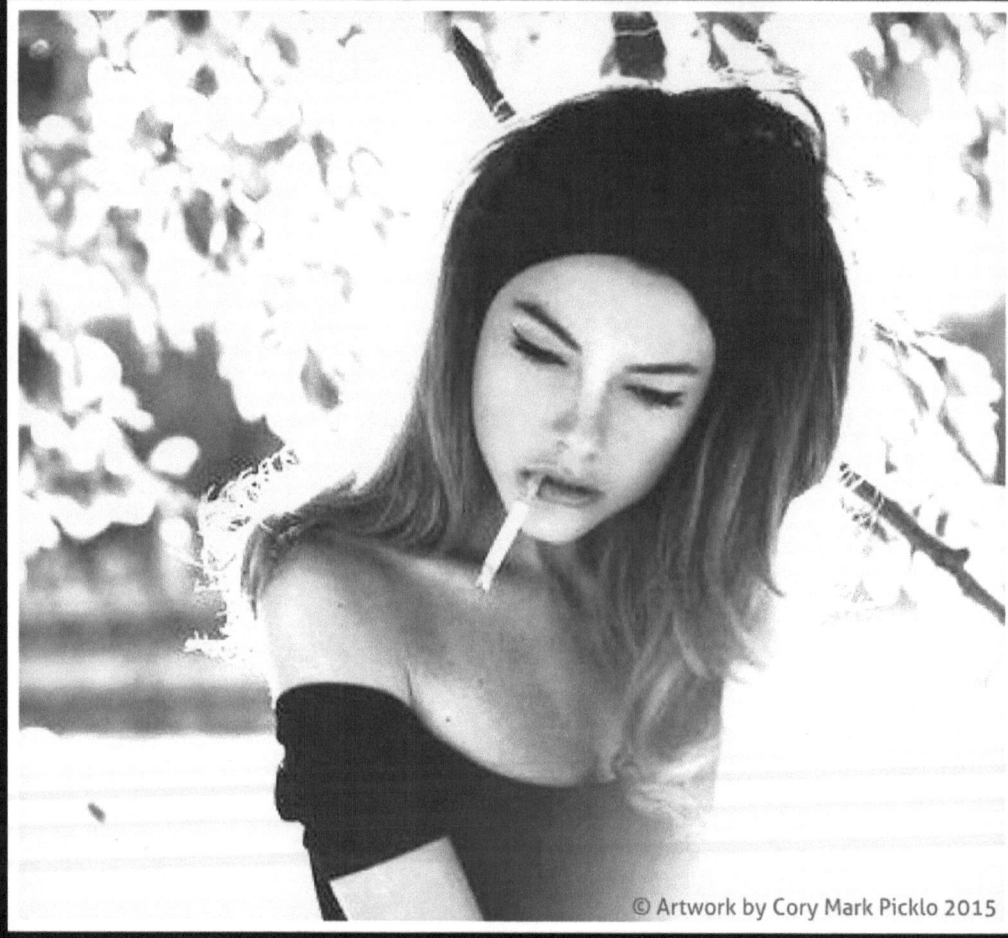

© Artwork by Cory Mark Picklo 2015

NATURAL BEAUTY Artwork by Cory Mark Picklo Photography by Creative Commons
P50

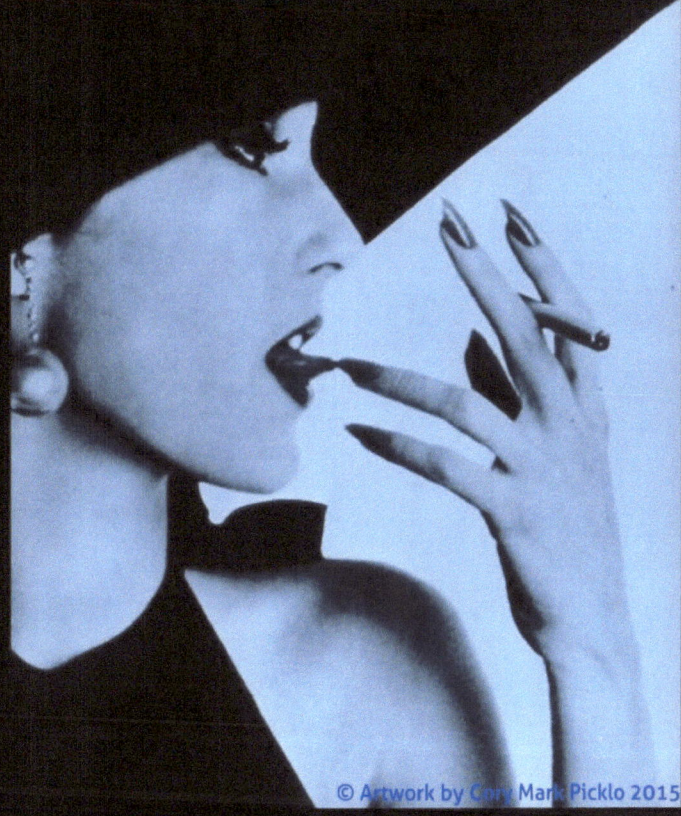

MISCHIEF Artwork by Cory Mark Picklo Photography by Creative Commons

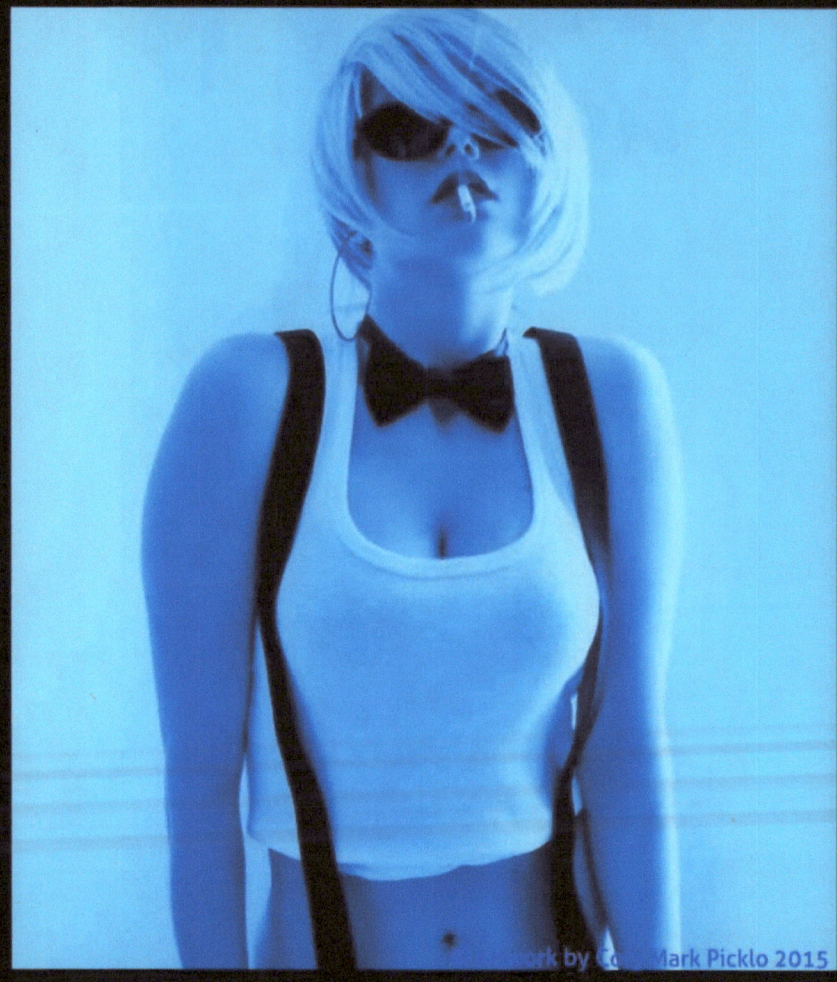

OVERTIME Artwork by Cory Mark Picklo Photography by Creative Commons

VI. Best Lighting

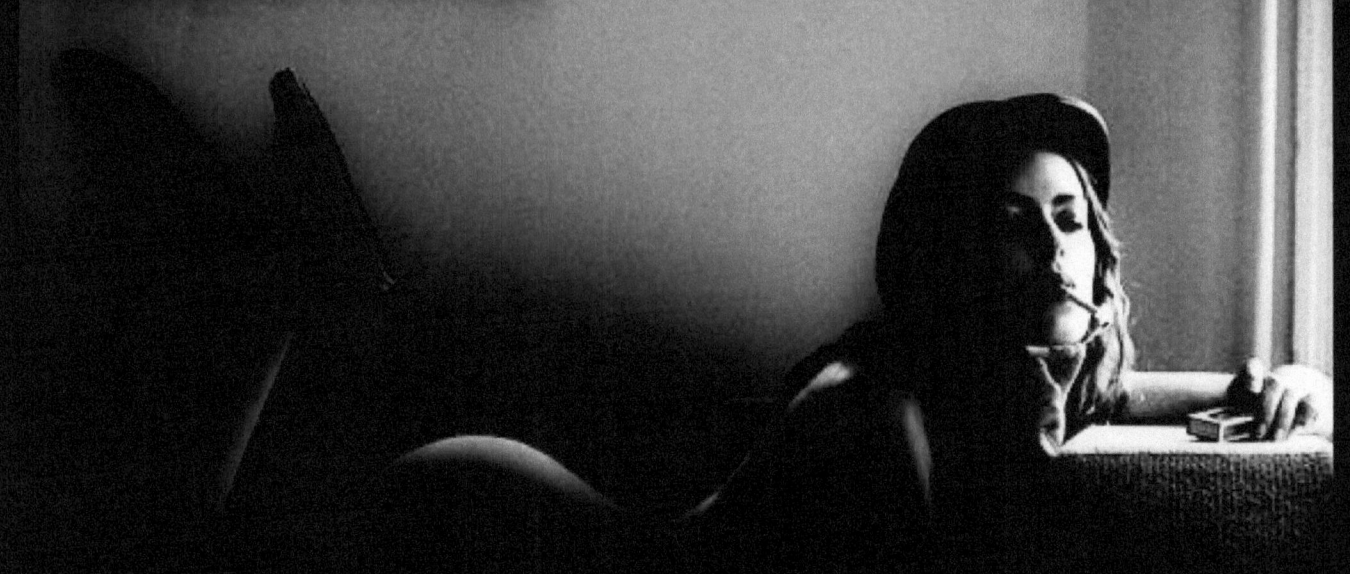

FREE Artwork by Cory Mark Picklo Photography by Creative Commons

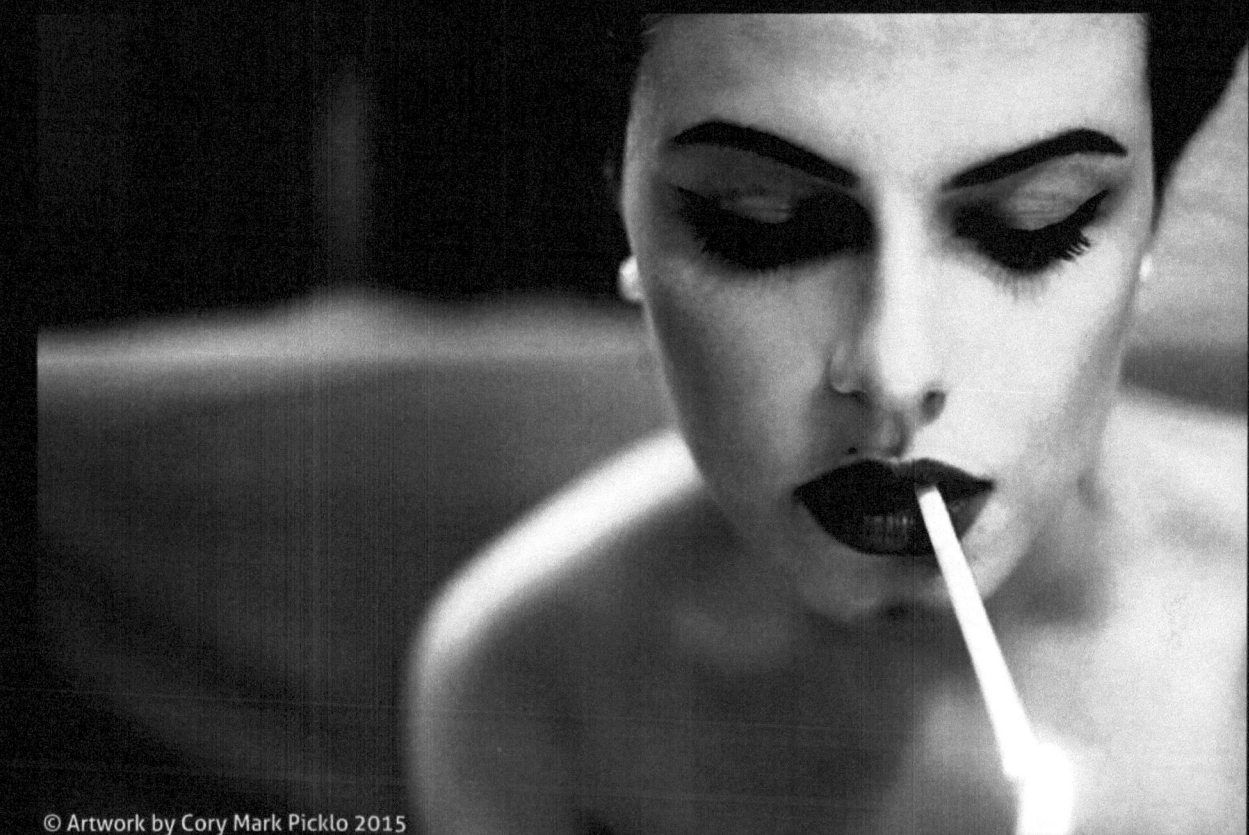

THE NIGHT IS YOUNG Artwork by Cory Mark Picklo Photography by Onanos

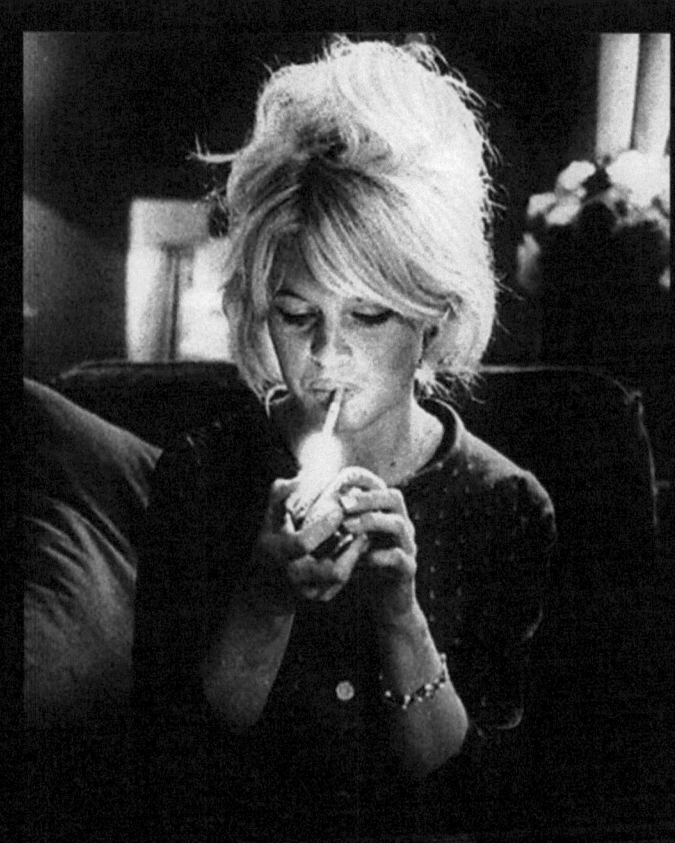

DELIGHT Artwork by Cory Mark Picklo Photography by Creative Commons

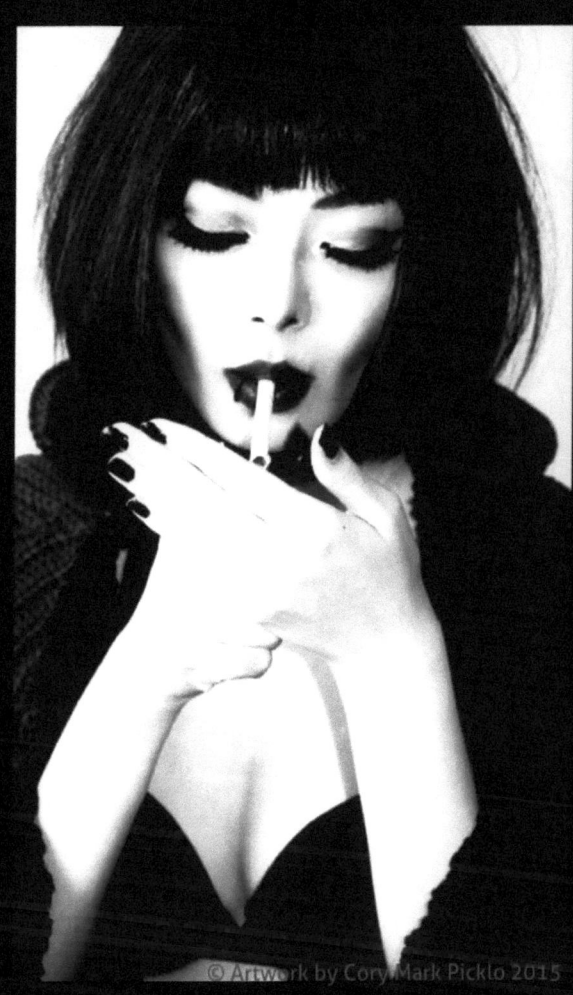

GOING PLACES Artwork by Cory Mark Picklo Photography by Creative Commons

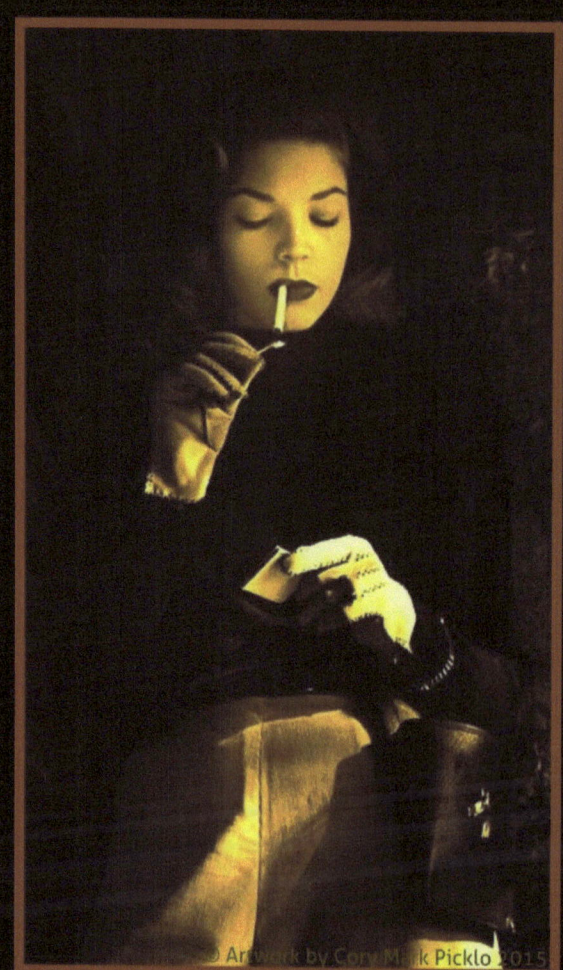

Lauren Bacall Artwork by Cory Mark Picklo Photography by Creative Commons

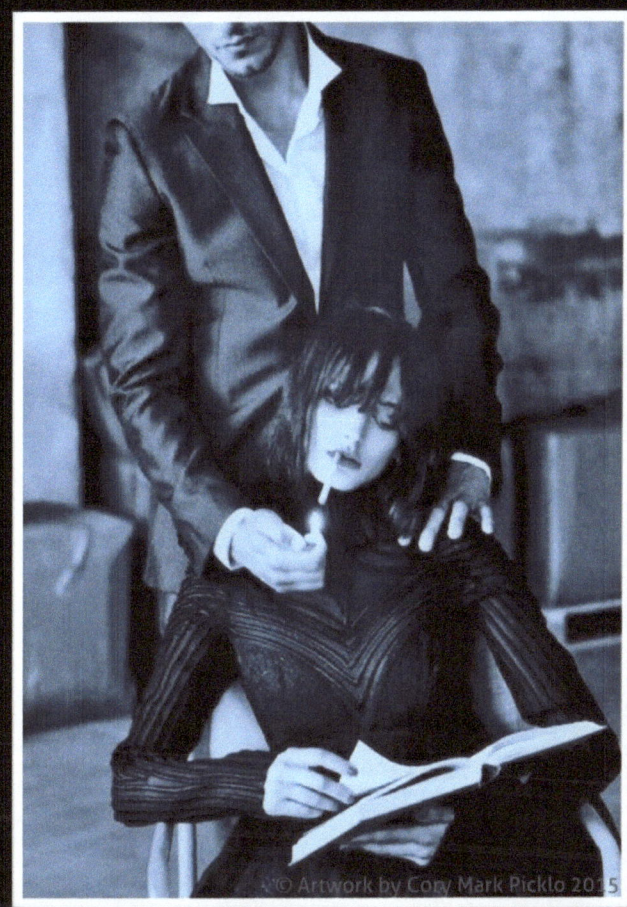

PLEASURE READING Artwork by Cory Mark Picklo Photography by Creative Commons

VII. Most Unique

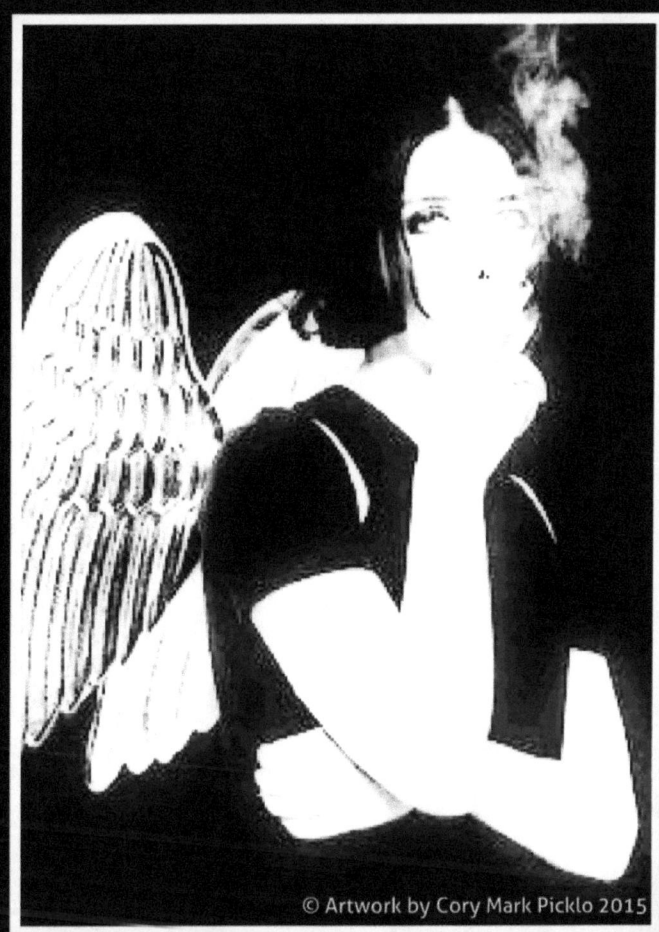

© Artwork by Cory Mark Picklo 2015

REAL ANGEL Artwork by Cory Mark Picklo Photography by Creative Commons

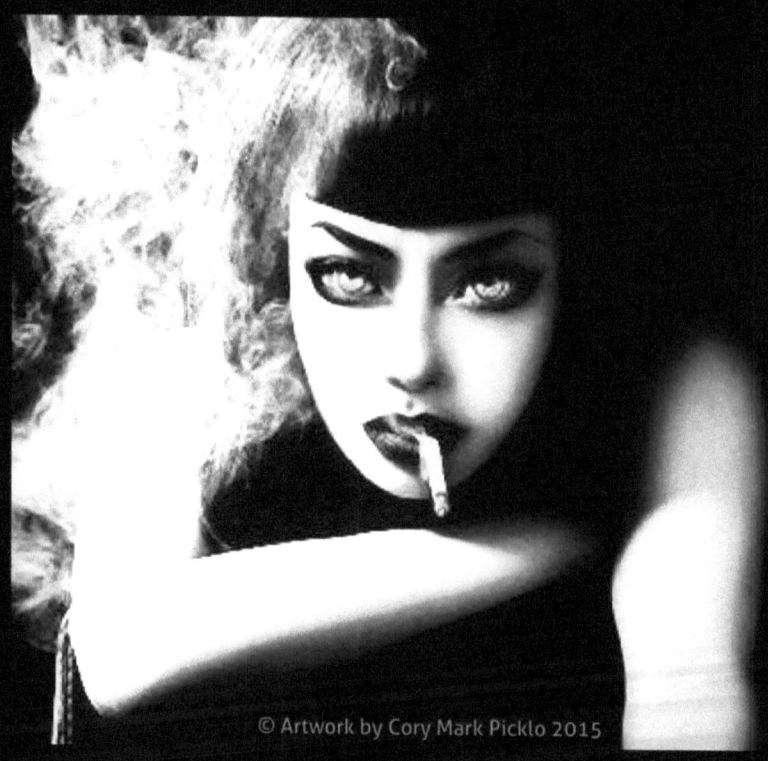

TAKE ME Artwork by Cory Mark Picklo Photography by Creative Commons

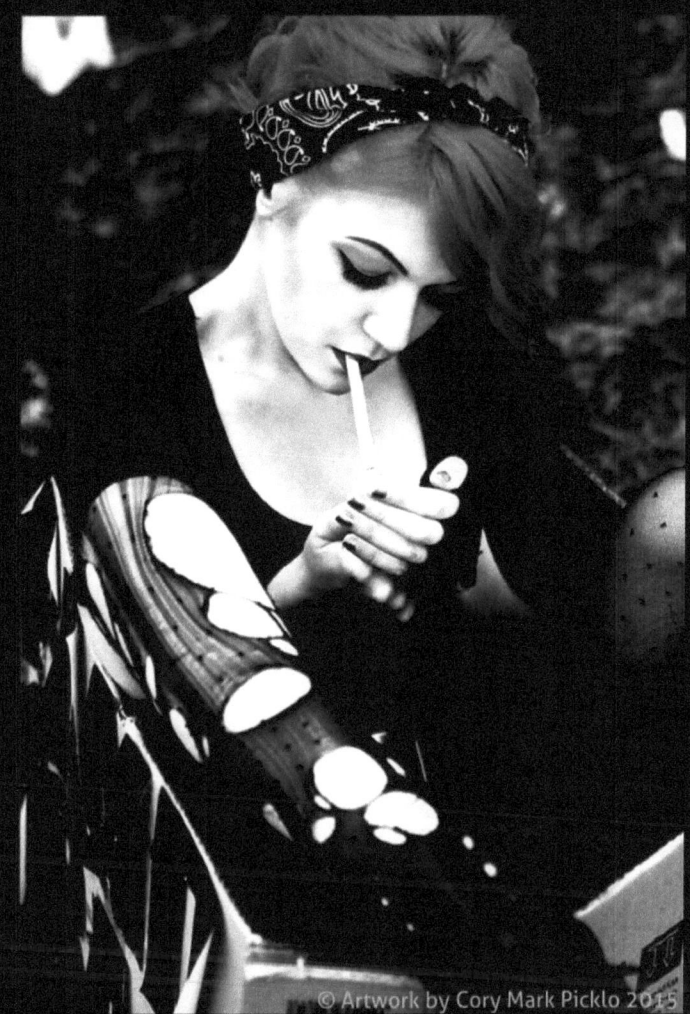

LIVING IN A BOX Artwork by Cory Mark Picklo Photography by Creative Commons

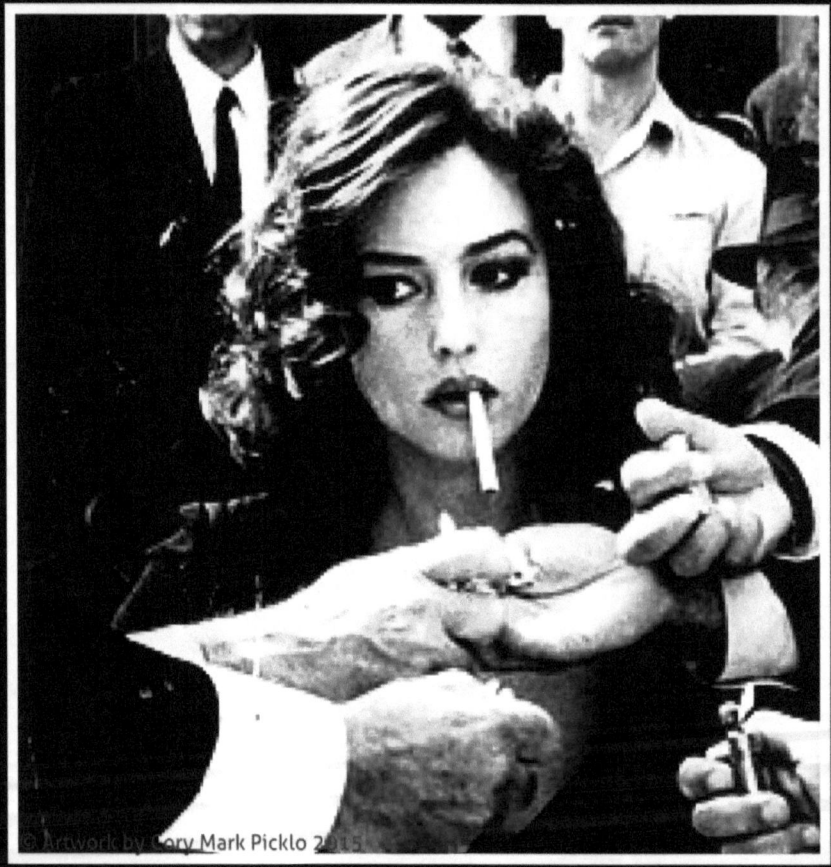

OVERWHELMING COURTESY   Artwork by Cory Mark Picklo Photography Malena

Greatest Women Poses
    with Cigarettes
    Galleria
        75 Years of Greatest Women Poses
50 Best 1940-2015

A c2cEverything Company

FIN

Another Fine Photo Collection by Cory Mark Picklo©2015

www.ingramcontent.com/pod-product-compliance
Lightning Source LLC
Chambersburg PA
CBHW050753180526
45159CB00003B/1443